TO

FROM

DATE

EVERYBODY ALWAYS
for kids

BOB GOFF

AND LINDSEY GOFF VIDUCICH

Illustrated by Diane Le Feyer

An Imprint of Thomas Nelson

Everybody, Always for Kids

Tommy Nelson, PO Box 141000, Nashville, TN 37214

Published in Nashville, Tennessee, by Tommy Nelson. Tommy Nelson is an imprint of Thomas Nelson. Thomas Nelson is a registered trademark of HarperCollins Christian Publishing, Inc.

The authors are represented by Alive Literary Agency, www.aliveliterary.com.

Tommy Nelson titles may be purchased in bulk for educational, business, fund-raising, or sales promotional use. For information, please email SpecialMarkets@ThomasNelson.com.

ISBN 978-1-4002-2087-8 (audiobook)
ISBN 978-1-4002-2086-1 (eBook)

Library of Congress Cataloging-in-Publication Data

Names: Goff, Bob, author. | Viducich, Lindsey Goff, author. | Le Feyer, Diane, illustrator. | Goff, Bob. Everybody, always.
Title: Everybody, always for kids / Bob Goff and Lindsey Goff Viducich ; illustrated Diane Le Feyer.
Description: Nashville, Tennessee, USA : Thomas Nelson, [2021] | Audience: Ages 6-10 | Summary: "A delightful call to live out the marvelous adventure of loving others, Everybody, Always for Kids draws kids into a collection of inspirational stories adapted from Bob Goff's New York Times bestseller Everybody, Always"-- Provided by publisher.
Identifiers: LCCN 2020034196 (print) | LCCN 2020034197 (ebook) | ISBN 9781400220830 | ISBN 9781400220878 (audiobook) | ISBN 9781400220861 (ebook)
Subjects: LCSH: Love--Religious aspects--Christianity--Juvenile literature. | Interpersonal relations--Religious aspects--Christianity--Juvenile literature.
Classification: LCC BV4639 .G62554 2021 (print) | LCC BV4639 (ebook) | DDC 248.8/2--dc23
LC record available at https://lccn.loc.gov/2020034196
LC ebook record available at https://lccn.loc.gov/2020034197

ISBN 978-1-4002-2083-0

Written by Bob Goff and Lindsey Goff Viducich

Illustrated by Diane Le Feyer

Printed in Korea

21 22 23 24 25 IMG 10 9 8 7 6 5 4 3 2 1

Mfr: IMG / Paju, Songunsa, Korea / January 2021 / PO #9589875

CONTENTS

CONTENTS

PROLOGUE

When I was a kid, I dreamed a lot about what I would be when I grew up. Do you do that too? The more I learned about the world and all the wonderful things you can make and do and see, the bigger my list of dreams grew. I wanted to be a pilot and a dad and an explorer, and I wanted to set the record for the number of ice cream scoops ever stacked on a cone. Eventually, my list was so long I figured it would be easier to make a short list of the few things I *didn't* want to do. That list included going for a swim in a pool with a hungry great white shark and discovering a lizard in my pocket (but now that I think about it, I kind of want to give those a try too).

Do you know what God's big dream is for us? It's not that we would be doctors or firefighters or writers or teachers or electricians or ice cream store owners—although I'm sure the world could always use a few more ice cream stores. Of all the terrific, helpful, creative things we could be, the most important thing God wants us to be is love.

It turns out that even when you're as old as me, you're not done learning. I used to think I could really impress God with all the things I did for Him. I even made a website to tell people about all the wonderful things I was doing for God.

I made a list of all the people I was helping and all the things I was doing to make their lives better, which is kind of silly when you think about it. Lately I've been learning that while I want to show God the lists of things I've done for Him, all He really wants to talk about is my heart and how much love is inside of it. God wants our hearts to overflow with love for Him and for all of the people He made.

The Bible talks a whole lot about loving others. In fact, this is one of the ideas Jesus talked about most when He was on earth. Jesus said that next to loving God, loving other people is

the most important thing we can do. When I first read that, I didn't think it seemed very hard. I love my family and my friends, and our neighbors are pretty easy to love too. They're really nice. I'm sure you have lots of people in your life who love you, and it's easy to love them right back, isn't it?

But what about that one girl who was mean to you on the playground last week? Or the boy in your class who is different from everyone else, and you don't really know how to talk to him? Or your baby sister who tears all your art projects off the refrigerator? Do we still have to love *them*—the people who hurt us, are different from us, or who we just plain don't understand?

I've been learning that when Jesus said He wants us to love others, He wasn't just talking about the people who love us back. God wants us to love *everybody*. What's more, He doesn't just want us to love them some of the time. He wants us to love them *always*. That's why I decided to call this book *Everybody, Always*. Can you image how silly it would be to call a book *Some People, Sometimes*? The truth is, I still find myself loving just some people, some of the time, so this is something I'm working on in my own heart—and I hope you'll decide to work on it too.

Becoming love doesn't mean that we need to give a special place in our lives to people who are unsafe. We need to use wisdom when we spend time with others. Your parents or other safe grown-ups in your life can help you figure out who is a safe person to spend time with. That said, though, we can make safe choices and still be loving to others.

The amazing thing about Jesus is that He didn't just tell us to love everybody—He *showed* us how to do this. Through His life, He showed us that He cares more about who is hurting than who is watching. He showed us ways to share what we have with a cheerful heart and in surprising and unexpected ways. He showed us that God's love is so big that no matter how many times we mess up, He loves us all the same. And do you know why God shows that love to us? It's so we can love everybody, always.

GO-KART RACE

When my kids were little, they got really into building go-karts. They would search the garage for any scrap wood they could find, and I would help them cut the boards. Then we'd find some wheels and attach them underneath the boards, making a platform that could roll. Next, we would cut more scrap wood to make seats, then paint them blue and green and attach them to the center of the platform. One of the kids figured out that if we attached a garbage can to the front of the go-kart, it would look like a real car, and we'd have a place for our feet to go. The whole thing could be steered by pushing the front axle back and forth with your feet. It was amazing, and the kids loved the building process and the ice cream we ate while we built.

None of our go-karts had an engine, because none of us could figure out how to put one on. That was okay, though, because one day we discovered that if we put a seat in the back, someone could sit facing backward and kick while the go-kart went down the hill—it worked just like an engine. This was our coolest go-kart design by far, and we couldn't wait to give it a try.

There was a pack of kids in the neighborhood who all

played together. They ranged in age from two to twelve, and I noticed that the twelve-year-old boys were always nice to my kids, who were the youngest. Even though my kids were a lot smaller, the older boys always made them feel included. One of the twelve-year-old boys treated my youngest son, Adam, who was two at the time, like a little sidekick. He kept a close eye out for him and made sure that Adam could join in any games the big kids were playing.

When the neighbor kids saw us pushing our trash-can go-karts up and down the street, they thought it looked like a whole lot of fun and decided they'd build go-karts too. They skipped the trash can on the front, but they figured out how to raise their go-karts on their wheels so they sat three feet off the street. The neighbors' go-karts could fly down the hill faster than anything we'd ever seen.

Every Saturday the neighborhood kids would strap on their brightly colored helmets and meet at the top of the hill to ride. One day my kids had an idea: What if we planned a race to celebrate all our cool go-karts and see how fast they could go?

When we stopped to think about who was racing, though, one of the twelve-year-old boys thought of something. "Wait," he said. "If we just race by pushing our carts with our legs, Adam won't have a chance to win!"

You see, Adam could push only so fast with his two-year-old legs. He didn't stand a chance against the big kids, and the other kids didn't want him to feel like he'd lost the race before it even started.

We decided to set up some extra challenges on the racetrack to solve this problem. The kids raced down the hill in their go-karts, but they had to stop at different stations along the way to do things like spin around ten times, eat a donut, throw a ball and catch it five times, and even make up a silly song. Instead of being a race focused on just running fast or steering straight, it also became a race of creativity, balance, catching, and how fast you could eat something delicious. When we made the race about everyone's talents, even the littlest kids had a fair chance to win.

A man named Paul wrote many letters to some of Jesus' first followers. Those followers were trying to figure out how to put their brand-new faith in Jesus into action. Paul wrote something like this: "If you want to follow Jesus in the way you live, here's how you do it—put aside your need to come in first place. Instead of looking to make yourself important, think about how you can make others feel important. Loving others like Jesus means that we're okay putting ourselves in last place."

Now, there's nothing wrong with competition or with winning. Winning is a lot of fun! But sometimes it's important to plan the race so everyone has what they need to be a part of it. It's important to be a kind winner and a kind loser, and sometimes we need to set aside the scoreboard and trophies altogether so that everyone can have a place in the game.

2

CAKE POPS

One day Jesus talked with His disciples about the types of people they should love. "It's easy to be loving toward people who love you," Jesus said. "Even people who don't know Me know how to do that! What I want you to do is to be nice to the people who aren't nice to you. That's how people will know you are different and that you're one of My followers."

I bet the disciples were confused by this. "Wait a second," I can picture them whispering to one another. "If someone hits us, shouldn't we be allowed to hit them back?" You see, that's what most people had learned, and it seemed fair to them. They thought if someone was mean to them, they had permission to be mean right back. But what Jesus wanted for His followers (and for us!) was something completely different.

Jesus talked about loving our *enemies*. To be honest, I can't think of anyone I would call an enemy. An enemy seems like someone I'd have a big fight with, but the truth is, I get along pretty well with most people. What I do have, though, are some folks who are just a little hard for me to be around. I disagree with them about some important things, and it seems like they're always saying something unkind when I see them. What do I do with people who I wouldn't call an enemy but who I just don't like very much?

Jesus wants us to love people in a way that is surprising, different, and unexpected. He wants us to love the people who aren't nice to us so that they will pause and wonder, *Why are they being so kind to me?*

Jesus' words got me thinking about the people I disagree with. When someone says something that hurts my feelings, my first idea is to say something mean back. But that isn't the different kind of love Jesus wants me to show others. So when my feelings are hurt these days, I do something different. Instead of thinking about how wrong the other person is and how right I am, I pick up my phone and order cake pops for them. It's true! I find the most exciting, sprinkle-covered cake pops I can and mail

them to the person I disagree with. Just thinking about how surprised they'll be to get cake pops in the mail makes me smile.

I've sent cake pops to dozens of people. The way I see it, people can disagree about a lot of things, but the minute you give someone a cake pop, you have something you can both agree on: cake pops are awesome. Who could disagree with that? Instead of talking about the things that make us different, we start talking about our favorite flavors and sprinkles. And who doesn't like talking about their favorite color of sprinkles?

The best part is what happens next: talking about sprinkles usually leads to talking about other things we like, about how we spend time with our families, or about books we've read and really enjoyed. I used to see only the things that made me different from a disagreeable person, and focusing on those things didn't help me like the other person very much. When you disagree with someone about something big, it can help to find something as small as a sprinkle to get you talking about what you have in common.

Cake pops are just one example, and I bet you could think of some other silly ideas too. It helps me to have a plan for something fun and surprising I'll do instead of fighting back or saying something unkind to someone who hasn't been nice

to me. Maybe it isn't cake pops for you, but perhaps you could give an encouraging note, a high five, or a stack of pancakes to someone who isn't very nice to you. Jesus said that when we only love people who love us, we won't stand out—and as His followers, He wants us to shine as bright as all of the sprinkles ever made!

Jesus said He doesn't just want us to be nice; He wants us to be *perfect*. And the only way we become perfect is by becoming love. It's going to take a lot of courage and patience to get there, and sometimes it might even involve a couple of cake pops!

3

MEETING CAROL

When our kids were little, we moved around a lot. Sweet Maria and I would buy a house that was pretty worn out, fix it up and sell it, then move on to a different house and do the same thing again. We loved doing projects together, and Sweet Maria loved making homes for our family.

One day the house right across the street from us went up for sale, and Sweet Maria and I knew it would be the perfect place for our family. We decided to finally stop moving houses and just stay in one spot. I really liked the idea of not having to pack any more boxes!

We haven't moved again since that day, so the last house we sold is still right across the street. Our family loved that house, and do you know what part of the house we loved most? The hallway! That house has the best hallway in the world. It runs right through the middle of the house and has doors at both ends and a door leading into each of the rooms on the sides. This meant the kids could close every single door and seal off the hallway, making a long, skinny, empty room. Our kids knew it was the perfect place to invent their next game. They closed all the doors, rounded up all the bounciest bouncy balls in the house, and started throwing the balls

around the hall. They bounced off of walls, doors, the floor, the ceiling, and even the kids. Nobody ever figured out how to score points, but that didn't stop them from playing. Hall Ball became our family's favorite game.

When it was time to sell our house and move across the street, we realized we weren't just picking a buyer for our house—we were picking a new neighbor! The first day the For Sale sign went up in our yard, five different people stopped by and said they were interested in buying our house. As we met with each of them, we asked ourselves, "Do we want them to be our neighbor?" One of the people we met was named Carol, and she was a widow in her fifties. She was so graceful and kind that love practically poured out of her.

We took Carol on a tour of the house, and the kids proudly showed her each room. They took Carol into the backyard and showed her the best place to find mud. Then they went inside, closed all the doors in the hallway, and showed Carol how to play Hall Ball—and they even let Carol win. After Carol thoughtfully inspected the house, she said with a broad smile, "I can tell this is a happy home. I would love to live here."

Over the decades that followed, Carol became a special part of our family and the entire neighborhood. The kids would run across the street to show Carol their art projects from school, and Carol would challenge them to a round of

Hall Ball. Carol loved monarch butterflies, and she showed the kids her collection of cups, plates, and rugs that were covered with images of the bright-orange wings.

Because Carol lived alone, I called almost every day to check in on her and ask how her day was going. She would tell me what she and her dog, Scout, had been up to that day, then she would fill me in on her latest adventures with the other ladies from the neighborhood. Our conversations were light and happy, and we loved having Carol as our neighbor.

One day, though, our conversation was a little different. When Carol answered the phone, she didn't sound like her usual happy self. I asked her what was wrong, and after a long pause, Carol said, "Bob, I just found out that I'm really sick. I have cancer." For the first time in our friendship, I could tell that Carol was afraid of something.

"Carol," I said, "I have an idea!"

I hung up the phone and raced to the store, where I bought two walkie-talkies. I set one up in our living room and one right next to Carol's bed. I told her she could call me on the walkie-talkie any time she started to feel afraid, and we checked in with each other every night. When Carol had to go to the hospital, I went to visit her and brought along our walkie-talkies. In the hallway, I found a kind nurse and asked her, "Will you give this walkie-talkie to Carol for me?"

I waited outside the curtain hiding Carol's bed and called her on the walkie-talkie. "Hello, Carol? Are you there?"

"Bob?" she called back after a moment. "Is that you?"

"Who else would it be?" We both threw our heads back and laughed.

The Bible says that when we love others, it chases fear away. At first, Carol was scared to face cancer, but when her family and friends gathered around her, she wasn't afraid anymore. The same thing is true about Jesus' love for us. Because He loves us perfectly and is always close to us, we don't have to be afraid anymore.

Lots of people talk about hearing from God when they feel afraid. They hear God saying comforting things to them, or they read comforting words in the Bible. I've usually found that God speaks to me through the people He's surrounded me with: my family, my friends, and my neighbors. When I need God's help or I'm feeling afraid, it seems like His answer is often to send me a friend to remind me I'm not alone and that God really, really loves me.

I think giving Carol a walkie-talkie reminded her that she didn't have to be afraid, because she wasn't alone—our family was right across the street, and God was close by too. The truth is, God is close by all of us, and sometimes this type of reminder can make all the difference.

4

CAROL'S PARADE

Our most special family holiday is New Year's Day. This surprises people because New Year's Day isn't normally a very big holiday for most families. But for us, we start looking forward to the next New Year's Day on January 2. We love the first day of the year because we spend it with our neighbors.

Every January 1, we decorate our street with more than one thousand brightly colored balloons, then we gather at the top of the hill and have a parade to celebrate the start of the new year. We've had this tradition for over twenty-five years, and every year hundreds of people meet us at the top of the street to walk in the parade together. Everyone is in the parade, and no one sits on the sides to watch.

Our street isn't very long, so the people at the front of the parade usually reach the end before the people at the back even start walking! We all just march past a couple of houses, then hang a right into our front yard to eat donuts together.

One of the most important parts of our parade tradition is crowning a new queen. Each year we'll ask one of the neighbors on our street to be the queen of the parade, and we'll have a brunch the day before the parade with all the former queens to celebrate the moment. We set a rose at every queen's plate, and all the ladies discuss their favorite memories from living on the street that year and welcome the new queen. As I bet you can guess, Carol was our queen one year, and when the day of the parade came, she proudly led us down the street.

Several years later, after Carol had gotten cancer and started to get better, she called me on the phone instead of on our walkie-talkies. "Bob," she told me, "the cancer is back." This time Carol was even sicker than before, and she knew she wouldn't get better. The doctor told her she had only a few more months to live.

At the end of the parade that year, instead of making a right turn into our front yard for donuts, the whole group made a left turn into Carol's yard. Carol sat in a chair in her living room, looking out the window, and the whole parade passed right by the window and blew her kisses through the glass. We all got to say good-bye and tell Carol how much we loved her, and she got to wave good-bye to everyone.

Each year, after the parade is over, another of our traditions is to collect the thousand helium balloons we blew up that morning and tie them all together. Usually we'll tie that massive bunch of balloons to one of the kids on our street and see if we can make them fly. The year the parade went

through Carol's yard, though, we did something a little different. Together with all the neighbors, we gathered up the balloons from the parade and tied them to Carol's house. My kids, who by that time were all grown up, ran up the hallway to Carol's room with another big bunch of balloons and tied them to her bed.

"We've been up to a little mischief, Carol," they told her with a laugh, and when Carol looked out her windows, all she could see were balloons.

Later that week, Carol went home to be with Jesus. I like to think that she had her second parade of the week. I'm not exactly sure what it will be like when we get to heaven, but I'm guessing it'll be a lot like the parade—everyone gathered with thousands of balloons, welcoming people to the neighborhood. When I get to heaven, I really hope I get to live across the street from Carol again.

The Bible is filled with little glimpses of what heaven will be like, but one thing in particular is repeated over and over—there won't be any fear or sadness in heaven. And the best part? We'll get to live with Jesus.

When Jesus was on earth, He taught about loving our neighbors. Even though Jesus really meant that He wants us to love everyone, no matter where they live, the truth is, I've often learned the most about love from my actual neighbors—the people who live on my street and who I see almost every day.

While we wait for heaven, we have a special job to do, and it's this: to love our neighbors. What do you think you could do to love the people near you? It might be a parade, or it might be something even better!

SKYDIVING

My son Adam is fearless. I bet you are too. Adam loves anything with an engine on it, and the faster it goes, the better. Over the years, Adam has picked up some pretty awesome hobbies. He flies airplanes and scuba dives. He sails boats and jumps off big cliffs. I always thought these things were crazy until I heard about his latest adventure: skydiving. When he goes skydiving, Adam jumps out of an airplane midair, falls for thousands of feet through the sky, then opens up a parachute to float the last little bit to the ground.

When I heard about Adam's new hobby, I asked him when his next jump would be and told him I'd love to come watch. What I didn't tell him, though, was that I had secretly been taking skydiving classes myself. When I arrived at the airport and found Adam suiting up with his parachute, I surprised him by putting on a parachute of my own.

"Dad, what are you doing?" Adam asked in disbelief.

"How hard could it be?" I asked with a wink.

We got into the airplane together and soared to thirteen thousand feet. At that point, someone opened the airplane's door, and the cabin was filled with the roar of rushing wind. I watched Adam run over to the door, and without hesitating,

he leapt from the plane. I've got to be honest: watching my son jump out of an airplane ahead of me, with only a tiny backpack strapped to his back, was more than a little unsettling. I was amazed at Adam's courage and sense of adventure. He jumped out of the plane like he had been doing it his whole life, like it was the most natural thing in the world.

As Adam jumped out, the strangest thing happened: I suddenly felt a strong urge to be *with* him in the air as he fell. I sprang to the door and threw myself out of the plane with all my strength. I jumped so hard, I jumped right out of my tennis shoes. No joke! You should try it. It's not easy to do, but it happens when you want to be *with* someone that much.

I love spending time with my kids, and that often means spending time doing the things they love to do. For Richard, that means going on motorcycle rides and helping him set up his living room for his next celebration. For Lindsey, it means spending time with her and her son, playing with toys over at our house. And for Adam, it means going on big adventures. Throughout the Bible, God calls Himself our dad and He calls us His kids. As a dad, this is special to me because thinking about how much I love spending time with my kids helps me to understand how much God loves spending time with me too.

Did you know that one of Jesus' names is Emmanuel? It means "God with us." Isn't that beautiful? The only reason I learned how to skydive and jumped out of my shoes was because I love Adam and I wanted to be with him. Sometimes loving others means doing things we wouldn't normally do so we can spend time with them. God wanted to be *with* us so much that He left heaven to spend time with us on earth (which, come to think of it, sounds an awful lot like skydiving!).

What I've learned from my kids is that loving others means taking the time to find out what activities they love to do. When you take the time to be with another person and do things together, you'll be surprised at how much you learn about yourself, your friends, and Jesus.

6

MY BUCKET

D o you have trouble being patient? Me too.

My daughter, Lindsey, is a teacher, and she told me about a beautiful book she read with her class about filling buckets. The idea is that everyone has an invisible bucket. When you say or do kind things for someone, you fill up that person's bucket. The goal is to be a person who fills up others' buckets with kind words and loving actions and encouragement. Isn't that just wonderful?

I started thinking about what I was filling others' buckets with and what I was filling my own bucket with. I realized that if I wanted to become love, I'd need to fill up my bucket with a whole lot of patience.

The book Lindsey read with her class *talked* about invisible buckets, but I'm someone who needs to learn by *doing*. So I went to Home Depot and bought a bucket. I decided to carry this bucket with me everywhere I went—to the grocery store, on airplanes, in my living room. I needed a constant reminder to fill my bucket with patience so that I could fill up others' buckets with kindness. I'm not going to lie; I got some pretty funny looks when I carried my bucket everywhere. It was a little embarrassing to get those funny looks, but I figured it

wasn't as embarrassing as letting my impatience problem get in the way of loving people.

I told Sweet Maria that I was practicing being more patient, and she said with a loving smile, "Bob, you're going to need a bigger bucket!" It was her kind way of telling me that I had some work to do.

One day I spoke at a church and brought my bucket along with me. I carried it up on stage and gave my whole talk with it sitting next to me. When it was time to go back to the airport, I got in my car, set the bucket on the seat next to me, and buckled it in. I was late for my flight and needed to drive fast, and I wanted to make sure my bucket of patience was safe.

When I finally arrived at the airport to return my rental car, I was in a big hurry, but the employee at the return center wasn't. I waited in a long line as the employee helped the cars in front of me at a snail's pace. When it was finally my turn, he slowly looked over my papers and checked in my keys. By this time, my flight was already boarding, and I knew if I didn't start running, I would surely miss it. The employee started chatting about the weather and asked how my trip went as he slowly printed my receipt. All the while, my foot was tapping, my fingers were drumming on the roof of the car, and I could feel all my patience starting to slip. I could feel some unkind words start to bubble up.

At that moment, I glanced down and saw the bucket next to me. *Fill it up with patience*, I told myself, and I swallowed hard so the impatient words wouldn't come flying out. After what seemed like an eternity, the rental car employee handed me my paperwork and said I was all good to go.

"How was your service today?" he asked with a smile.

I looked at my bucket again and thought for a moment before responding. Some not-very-patient words ran through

my mind. I took a deep breath, though, and told myself again, *Fill your bucket with patience.*

"It was terrific! Thanks!" I said with a smile as I gathered up my bucket and bags. I knew I'd missed my flight, so I walked a bit more slowly toward the terminal, knowing I would need to find another way home.

Just then I heard the rental car agent call after me, "Hey, Bob!"

I turned around, surprised. "Yes?" I asked.

"That was a great sermon this morning."

I felt my heart skip a beat while I took in what he just said. "Were you at church this morning?" I asked as my jaw dropped.

"Yeah!" the man replied cheerfully. "I really liked what you said about patience!"

I felt shocked and relieved all at the same time. Can you imagine what would have happened if I *hadn't* been patient? That day I learned that you can use the best words in the world to *talk about* what you believe, but what people are really watching is what you *do.* And sometimes you might not even realize people are watching!

I don't carry my bucket around as much anymore, but I do keep it in my office where I can see it. I figured out that for me, having something silly like a bucket sitting around can help me remember a lesson that God is still teaching me. You might not need a bucket to remind yourself to be patient and kind, but whatever you do, make sure your actions *show* people that you love them, even when things don't go the way you wanted.

7

BUILDING SCHOOLS

One of the commandments in the Bible is to love our neighbors as we love ourselves.

Wait. Love *ourselves*?

That's right! Think about the things you do to take care of yourself—the things you do to make yourself feel good, safe, and happy. If you're sick, you go to the doctor to get medicine. You celebrate your birthday with friends and family. You eat good food so your body grows strong and you have the energy you need to focus at school. These are all great things, and they're part of showing ourselves love.

All the things that help us feel loved and cared for are the same things Jesus wants us to give to others too. Loving others means that we want for them all the good things that we want for ourselves.

Try this: Make a list of all your favorite things—the things you are most thankful for. You might put family, friends, games, places, toys, pets, school, and food on that list. Now think about the people in your life. What are some ways that you could share some of the same things you love with others?

How could you help your little sister experience the same

feeling you have when you play with your favorite toy? How could you help the kids in your class who don't have many friends, knowing that a friend is what they need most? When we really love others as ourselves, we're saying that the things someone else wants and needs are just as important to us as the things we want and need.

Both Sweet Maria and I really struggled at school growing up, and maybe that's true for you too. Even though school was hard for us, as we got older, we saw how important education is.

In some countries in the world, there are people who say that little girls shouldn't go to school. You and I both know that isn't right. Every country in the world needs boys *and* girls who will grow up to be strong leaders, and all children should be able to go to school.

I learned about some young girls in a country called Afghanistan who didn't have a school to go to, even though they really wanted one. These little girls wanted to learn how to read. I remembered how much my own kids wanted to learn to read when they

were young and how much I wanted that for them, and I knew it wasn't right for the girls in Afghanistan to be kept out of school. Loving others like I love myself means caring about the Afghan girls' education just like I care about my own kids having a school to go to. At first, I wasn't really sure what to do, but then I became friends with a terrific young leader in Afghanistan who saw this same problem. We decided to work together to do something about it.

Not long ago we opened the doors to a new school for girls in Afghanistan. And get this—the building where the school meets looks just like a cupcake! Isn't that great? In a country where many girls aren't allowed to learn how to read, there's now a group of girls walking into a bright, beautiful build- ing each day to learn their letters and numbers from great teachers. Those little girls and their teachers are some of the bravest people I know.

As you go about your day, keep adding to the list of things you love to do and the things you are thankful to have. When we pay attention to the things we love, it can help us remember that those things are important to others too. And then we can love others like we love ourselves.

8

THE SWIMMER

O ur family has a home in the mountains of Canada that's right by the water. We call it the Lodge. At the Lodge, all of the roads are carved into the side of a mountain. No matter where you go, you'll find a steep hill going up the mountain on one side of the road and a steep cliff dropping straight into the water on the other side. The roads are nice and wide, but we drive very carefully! The cars we drive on the roads are called Rhinos, and they're like golf carts with huge wheels.

One day my son Richard was driving on one of the roads, and he parked the Rhino when it was time for lunch. He pulled over to the side of the road, on the uphill side away from the cliff, but he forgot one important step: he didn't turn the steering wheel. You're probably a few years away from driving, so let me give you your first driving lesson. When you park on a hill, it's a good idea to turn your steering wheel so that if your car starts to roll down the hill without you in it, it will roll into the curb and stop instead of roll out into the street and down the hill. Up at the Lodge, there are no curbs, so we turn the wheel so that if a Rhino gets loose, it will turn to the uphill side of the road and stop. That day, though, Richard forgot, and he accidentally left the Rhino aimed at the other side of the road—the side with the cliff!

Later that day, Richard walked back to the place where he left the Rhino, but he couldn't find it anywhere. Richard shook his head as he walked up and down the road, wondering if there had been a landslide or if a bear had stolen the car. How could a Rhino just disappear?

Then he saw them.

Oh no! Richard thought as looked down at the fresh tire tracks. Can you guess where they led? *Right off the cliff.*

Richard felt awful. He was the kind of kid who took great care of things. He would never do something like this on purpose, and it was a big, expensive mistake.

As Richard choked out his story of what had happened to the Rhino, I knew I had to choose my first words carefully.

"Son," I said, "I forgive you."

Words have power, and those words were exactly what Richard needed to hear. To be honest, I was pretty upset that the Rhino had gone off the cliff. In moments like those, it's hard for me not to use harsh words. What I've been learning, though, is that loving people means loving them *always*, even in moments when I'm disappointed or frustrated. The truth is, Rhinos can be fixed and replaced, but I only have one relationship with my son.

What happened next was amazing. Do you know how to rescue big, heavy things from the bottom of the ocean? Scuba divers dive down with huge, empty balloons, tie them to whatever sank, and then fill up the balloons with air while they're underwater. Just as balloons with helium float in air, balloons filled with air float in water, and the balloons lift

the object up to the surface. We called some scuba divers to help us with the Rhino, and they went underwater while we waited at the surface. Suddenly, the Rhino burst through the waves, pulled by a giant white balloon! We clapped and cheered and pulled the Rhino to shore. With a little work, the Rhino was soon back up and running again after its dive into the ocean. On that day, we gave the car a new nickname:

the Swimmer. Some of the Swimmer's metal bars are a little bent now, and it sometimes turns to the side a little all on its own, but we still drive it around the Lodge's roads to this day, over ten years later!

In our relationships, sometimes we're a little bit like Richard, sometimes we're like the Swimmer, and sometimes we're the balloons. We all make mistakes and can feel awful, just like Richard did after he forgot to turn the wheels when he parked. Other times, someone else makes a mistake that makes us feel like we've sunk to the bottom, just like the Rhino in the water. And sometimes we see people who are hurt or who have made a mistake, and we get to be like the balloons that pull them back up. Every time I drive the Swimmer, I remember that Jesus loves both the people who are hurting and the ones who hurt them, and He always wants to bring those people back up.

9

CONNECTING
THE DOTS

When I was little, I was covered in freckles. I had so many freckles, it sometimes seemed like my freckles had freckles. I had freckles on my nose and cheeks, down my arms, and peeking out from under my socks.

Having freckles wasn't so bad. In fact, I don't think I would have given them much thought if others didn't. But when I stepped foot on the playground my first day of school and heard, "Hey, you! Spot!" I realized for the first time there was something about me others might not like—something that made me different. It's a pretty crummy feeling, isn't it?

My Grandma Mary was one of my best friends when I was growing up, and I knew she'd be a great person to talk to. It's always a good idea to let a safe grown-up know when you're feeling sad. As I told her about how the kids at school called me Spot, my eyes welled up with tears. "I wish I didn't even have freckles," I cried.

Grandma Mary looked at me with love and said, "I'm so sorry, Bob. Those kids shouldn't have said that to you."

She paused for a long, thoughtful moment and said, "Hold on a minute. There's something I want to show you."

Grandma Mary disappeared for a minute and returned with a marker. She took my hand in hers and pulled my arm up so it was close to her face. "Let's see what we can find here," she said playfully, and she started connecting the dots. I watched in amazement as my arm became filled with animals, cars, houses, and sailboats. I had a whole parade of animals on my arm, and I didn't even know it!

"See?" Grandma Mary asked, her eyes twinkling. "Those freckles are one of the best things about you. Those other kids might only see spots, but what I see is artwork!"

Suddenly, my freckles didn't bother me at all. In fact, I thought they were pretty cool! Seeing myself through the eyes of someone who loved me helped me see something special in myself—something I wouldn't have noticed otherwise.

What I've learned is that the people who only see your spots are often the people who have lots of hurts inside. But Jesus wants us to see people in a different way—in a way that encourages others. He talked a lot about people who were poor or sick or unpopular because they looked different, and He said they were exactly the kinds of people who belonged in His kingdom. Jesus also wants His kingdom filled with

dot-connectors just like you—people who see the "spots" in others as beautiful works of art.

Be on the lookout for ways you can see the art in someone else! And when you do, be sure to tell them. As a person who is becoming love, you can be someone who tells people who they are.

You're a great friend.

You don't give up when something is hard for you.

I love you just because you're you!

Every time we encourage others, we help build Jesus' kingdom here on earth.

10

BE AVAILABLE

"Bob here! How can I be helpful?"

That's how I've been answering my phone these days. Truth be told, I spend an amazing number of minutes each day on the phone. It rings so often I sometimes think I hear it even when it isn't ringing, like when you get a song stuck in your head. I get calls all day long from the most wonderful people. Sometimes they're a group of high school kids with their youth group leader, sometimes the calls are from grandparents, and sometimes kids call me with their parents. I can barely get anything done because my phone rings so much, and I wouldn't change a thing.

You see, when I wrote my very first book for grown-ups, I thought it would be nice to let people know how they could get ahold of me. Writing a book is a little like writing a big, long letter to your readers, and lots of authors like to give their readers an address where they can write back. It's special to hear from people after you've worked on something for them for a long time, and I love hearing how our family's stories have encouraged other families to do special things too.

The thing about letters, though, is that they can take a long time to arrive, and you already know I have trouble being patient. I love to talk to people, so I had a terrific idea. What if I put my phone number in the back of the book, so people could call me anytime they wanted to talk about what they read?

Something funny and unexpected happened. While I had guessed that just a few people would buy the book with my phone number in it, it turned out that about a million people ended up with a copy! That's a lot of people, which means a lot of phone calls.

Even though all the calls mean I am constantly being interrupted, I'm learning the importance of making myself

available to people. That's something Jesus did while He was here on earth, especially when He was teaching. He was always with people, and He seemed to have unending patience with people who stopped Him to ask a question or ask for help. It didn't matter who the people were—kids or grandparents, healthy people or sick people—Jesus made time for all of them.

Now, your parents probably wouldn't like it very much if you handed out their phone numbers without permission. But I bet you can think of ways that you could be more available to other people at home and at school. Maybe your little sister interrupts you when you are trying to read a book because she wants to play. Or maybe you've moved on to free time in class while some friends are still finishing their work, and they ask you for help. Could you make yourself available to others? Try answering them like this: "I'm here! How can I be helpful?" Then see what happens. You might be amazed at how much you can make another person feel loved by simply being available to help or spend time with them. And the more you do it, the more you'll see that becoming available helps you become a little more like Jesus.

11

HOLES IN MY POCKETS

Earlier I told you about a man named Paul who wrote lots of letters to churches and explained to them how their lives would look different now that they were following Jesus. Many of those letters became part of the Bible, so we get to read them and learn from them too! In one of his letters, Paul wrote that following Jesus is like becoming a completely new person. Paul described becoming new as something you put on, like a fresh change of clothes after you've been playing outside. You take off the old self that had anger, greed, mean thoughts, and maybe some not-so-nice words, just like you take off clothes when they get dirty. Then you put on a whole new self, just like putting on new, clean clothes. Paul said that putting on the new self means putting on things like gentleness and kindness and forgiveness. This new self is the person we get to be because of Jesus.

A couple of years ago I realized I was carrying around a lot of extra things I didn't really need or want. These weren't the kinds of things you carry in your arms, but rather the kinds of things you can't see but carry in your heart. For example,

I was holding on to some grudges—that's when you stay mad at people when they've done something wrong in the past. Grudges are heavy in their own kind of way. Holding on to grudges made me feel grumpy and frustrated—actually, it's kind of the same feeling you experience when you have a pebble in your shoe that keeps bothering you. I needed to learn how to let those things go.

One day I went to put my keys in my pants pocket and was surprised when I heard them fall to the ground with a loud clatter. "What in the world is wrong with my pants?" I asked Sweet Maria. I looked behind me and realized I had a whole trail of items, like I'd tossed confetti in the air and ran. Receipts, coins, paper clips, keys. Everything I had put in my pockets that day was scattered all around the house. When I took a closer look, I realized I had a huge hole in my pocket!

The hole in my pocket got me thinking. If wearing pants with a big ol' hole in the pocket made it easy for me to lose my keys, maybe I could treat grudges the same way. Instead of holding on to a grudge that wasn't any good for me—or

for the person who had made me mad so long before—maybe I could just let that grudge slip away behind me, and everyone would feel a whole lot lighter!

To remind myself to let go of grudges, I grabbed a pair of scissors and started chopping away at my pants pockets. Maybe having big holes in all my pants would remind me to let go of grudges. And you know what? It worked! Now every time I put something in my pocket, I hear the clatter of keys or coins or paper clips falling to the ground, and I remember to let go of things in my heart that aren't good for me or the people in my life.

Putting on my holey pants each morning reminds me that I'm putting on a new person, and that new person can't hold on to anything that isn't the good stuff God wants for me.

Now, you shouldn't start cutting holes in your clothes without your parents' permission, but when you get ready for school tomorrow morning, don't just think about the clothes you are putting on. Think about the new person God is making you into—the person who is becoming love. Put on the gentleness, kindness, and forgiveness that show others the new person God has made you into.

12

A WELCOME FROM WALTER

Welcome to San Diego International Airport," the loud-speaker blared. Crowds shuffled through the noisy, crowded airport, moving toward the baggage claim area. There were cheers and hugs and smiles as arriving passengers were greeted by their families and friends. One family in the crowd of passengers looked around nervously. They had just arrived in the United States for the first time and were exhausted from their trip.

Suddenly, a bright, beaming face pushed through the crowd in the arrivals area, waving a welcome sign and carrying balloons. "Friends! Welcome!" Walter called. And before the family knew it, they were all caught in a big hug from Walter. You see, my friend Walter knew exactly what it felt like to have to move to a new country.

People move to the United States for a lot of wonderful reasons. Some people move because they want to go to school or were hired for a new job. Some people want to live in a new country just for fun, and some people move to the United States to be close to family.

Sometimes, though, people move to the United States for sad reasons. You wouldn't guess this because of his big smile, but Walter had to leave his own country because it wasn't safe for him to be there anymore. There was a war, and he was really worried he might get hurt. So Walter made a new home in the United States. This is called being a refugee.

Walter moved here and got settled in, but he didn't forget about where he came from. Walter knew there were lots of other people like him who moved to the United States from countries that were unsafe. New families arrived each day after facing hunger, thirst, and hard times. When these refugees arrived in the airport, they often didn't have any bags with them. Just like Walter, they had been forced to leave their countries with only their clothes on their backs.

Walter understood how scared these refugees would feel when they arrived in a new place, so he decided to start welcoming them. When the families got off their planes and walked nervously through the airport, Walter was right there with his bright smile and arms outstretched for a hug. "Welcome!" Walter would shout joyfully. "I'm so happy you're here!"

I've gone with Walter a few times to meet people at the airport, and I always bring balloons with me. I think balloons are a great idea for any occasion—from shopping at the grocery store to an appointment with the dentist—and I've noticed that big smiles and brightly colored balloons mean the same thing to everyone, even if you don't speak the same language. They mean welcome and celebration.

Jesus once taught His disciples something important about welcoming others. "Do you know," Jesus asked His disciples, "that every time you do something for someone who is hungry or thirsty or who needs clothing or shelter, you really do that thing for Me?"

When someone does something nice for one of my three kids, I feel like they've done that nice thing for me. Jesus said that God is our dad, and when we treat His kids kindly, it's like we've done that kind thing for God.

I'm not sure what it will be like when we first get to heaven, but I wonder if it will feel a lot like Walter's welcomes at the airport. If I had to guess, I bet Jesus will be standing there at the entrance, holding a fistful of colorful balloons, welcoming us with a huge smile and ready to celebrate the ways we showed love to Him by showing love to others.

13

TWO-BUNK JOHN

J ohn, what if you spin the globe, put your finger down, and see where it lands?" I asked.

I was talking with my friend John, who was one of the students in a college class I taught. "I don't know what I should do after I graduate," John had said. "I want to do something to help people, but I don't know where to go."

John had invited me to come over to his house, and we were sitting together on the back porch. He and a group of friends met at their house every Friday night to talk about their faith and how they could put it into action. What I loved about John and his friends was that they didn't want to just talk about their faith—they wanted to do something.

As you grow up, you'll have a lot of big transitions in your life. You'll move from elementary school to middle school, then from middle school to high school. After graduating from high school, you might decide to go to college, or you might get a job. You might stay close to home, or you might move far away. You'll get to make many decisions about the wonderful things you can do with your life. As I sat with John, he told me he was trying to decide what to do after college. Should he get a job? Should he go back to school again?

Eventually, John and I decided that we would start a school together in a country called Uganda, and he would move there to get everything started. We had heard about kids in northern Uganda who didn't have a school because of a war in their country, and the kids really needed and wanted a place to learn.

John moved to Uganda and started working on the school. As the months went by, John called me a lot. I always tried to answer the phone before the first ring was done because I knew he would have something awesome to share about the new school. But one day John called about a problem. "Bob," he said, "we need a bunk bed at the school. There are two boys who walk eight miles every day to get to school, and they need a place to stay so they don't have to walk so far."

We just had one little problem with this idea—our school building was small and simple, with just three classrooms and not much else.

"John," I said, "I just don't think we have room for a bunk bed at the school. Plus, how would we feed the boys if they don't go home after class is done?"

"I can figure it out, Bob!" John replied cheerfully, already forming a plan in his mind. "Just two bunks are all we need!"

Several years have passed since that phone call, and do you know what happened? We now have more classrooms at our school—and a lot more bunks! In fact, there are now three whole buildings full of bunk beds.

John and I didn't know the whole plan when we started, but here's the beautiful thing: right as the school was starting to grow, I wrote my first book. Sweet Maria and I decided to do something special with the money we earned from the book—we'd use it to build more school buildings and buy more bunk beds! What started out as two little bunks quickly became something much bigger.

It wasn't easy to get the school set up for kids to live there. In addition to figuring out how to build buildings and buy beds and make sure those places were safe, we had to find great teachers to live at the school to teach and care for the kids. It was a lot of work, but when John got his two bunks, his creative idea for how to show love toward others spread quickly and grew. Many people were inspired to jump in and help us make it happen, and they did! To this day, the kids at the school call John "Uncle John," but to me he'll always be Two-Bunk John.

Two-Bunk John reminds me of a story about Jesus. One day Jesus and His disciples were in a place far away from any towns, and a big crowd of people gathered around Him to hear Him teach. As the day passed, people started to get hungry.

"Jesus," the disciples said, "we're in the middle of nowhere,

and everyone is getting hungry. You should send this crowd away so they can go back to town and buy some food."

Jesus' response to the disciples surprised them. "You should give them something to eat!" I can imagine the disciples must have felt confused, and Jesus must have smiled because He knew exactly what to do.

"Bring Me what you have," Jesus said. The disciples searched around and found a boy in the crowd who had packed a meal with five small loaves of bread and two fish and was willing to share.

Jesus thanked God for the food, and the disciples started passing it around the crowd. Then something miraculous happened— no matter how many people broke off pieces of bread and fish, the food never ran out. Everyone in the large crowd ate until they were full, and there was even food left over! God took a small act of generosity and made it grow until it was enough to feed thousands.

When one boy shared some bread and fish, Jesus used it to feed a crowd.

When John bought a couple of bunk beds, God turned a school into a home for hundreds of children.

When it comes to loving others, no act of love is too small. In the kingdom of God, Jesus can use even our smallest acts of generosity and multiply them to show love to thousands!

14
CHEERFUL GIVERS

My friend Doug loved Jesus, and he spent his days talking with people about the things Jesus taught. Doug didn't just talk about loving Jesus, though. He lived like Jesus.

If someone complimented something Doug was wearing—say, his watch or his shirt or his tie—he'd quietly slip it off and give it to them. Anything Doug had that another person really liked, he'd share on the spot.

When Jesus was on earth, He taught people about the same kind of sharing that Doug did. One of the places people could share with others was at the temple, where people came to worship God and give offerings. Maybe you've seen this happen in your church, when a bag or a basket is passed around and people drop money in it. Offerings are used to help the church take care of people, like buying food or clothes for people who need it. A lot of people like to give offerings as a way to thank God for everything He has given us. God has given us so many good things, and we get to celebrate those things by sharing with others!

Jesus was sitting in the temple one day when He noticed something strange. Some of the people who arrived brought big, expensive gifts for God. They made sure everyone saw what they were doing by wearing their fanciest clothes and making a big deal out of how much they were giving to God. Those people thought that if everyone saw them giving big offerings to God, they would be special. You and I know how silly that sounds, and Jesus thought so too.

As He continued to watch people bring their offerings, Jesus saw an old woman walk into the temple. She was dressed in worn-out clothes and looked a little hungry. The woman clearly didn't have very much money. Jesus saw her quietly walk toward the front of the temple and pull two small coins out of her pocket. She carefully placed them with the bigger, fancier gifts, then quietly slipped back into the crowd.

Most people wouldn't have noticed the woman, but her small act of love wasn't missed by Jesus. He always seemed to see little things like that. Jesus turned to His disciples. "Friends, did you see that? Listen closely, because I'm telling you the truth—those two small coins are worth more than all the big and fancy gifts other people gave. The people who were trying to get our attention were giving out of their wealth, but this woman gave up money she really needed to honor God and help someone else."

Something that's easy to forget is that everything in the world is *already God's*. God is the Creator and owner of everything, and He doesn't need our offerings to do good in the world. In fact, God doesn't even really look at our gifts when we give them. He looks at our *hearts*. You know that excited feeling you get when you plan a special surprise present for someone in your family on their birthday? God loves to see His kids excited about giving to others, no matter what the gift is.

When I think about Doug giving his favorite tie to someone who admired it, and the woman giving her offering at the temple, it makes me think differently about the things I have. What I'm learning is that when we are becoming love, we are generous with what we have—and it's not about how much we give but about giving with a generous heart. When we are becoming love, we don't make a list of all the things we give to others. We know that everything we have is God's to begin with, and what Jesus cares about most is our hearts.

15

THE PIZZA PLACE

D ing ding ding ding ding!

The alarm announcing the winner of the game rang through the room, joining the other dings, bells, and music of the arcade machines lining the walls. When the kids were growing up, we had a favorite pizza place around the corner from our house, and it was filled with more noise than I'd ever heard in my life. Noise was the thing the pizza place made best, even better than the pizza itself. We were never interested in the pizza anyway. We were there for the tickets.

Maybe you've played an arcade game like this before: You trade real money for a pile of game tokens, and you put a token in a game slot to play. Each time you win a game, a bell rings or a song plays to congratulate you, and tickets come shooting out of the machine. The better you are at the game, the more tickets you win, and the more tickets you win, the more options you have when you go to the prize counter.

We liked all the games in the pizza place, but our favorite by far was Skee-Ball. We got pretty good at it. In that game, you roll wooden balls up a ramp and win tickets by landing them in different spots. My favorite part of Skee-Ball was that you got three balls per token, so you could win a lot of tickets if you had good aim.

After running out of tokens, we would take our tickets to the prize counter. One of the walls in the noisy, crowded game room was filled with the most amazing prizes you could imagine. Huge stuffed animals, dolls, and race cars lined the shelves. Each prize was worth a different number of tickets, and if you had enough tickets, you could trade them in for a prize.

One day the kids had an idea. "What if we saved our tickets for a really big prize, rather than trading them in now?" they asked. On the drive home, I heard the kids discussing all the big things they could save up for. They were pretty sure even bigger prizes were in the back room—like a pet dinosaur or a jumbo dunk tank.

We saved our tickets for weeks. "We're going to get one of everything!" the kids told each other. We kept the tickets in a shoe box and counted them after every visit. We had thousands.

When the day finally came to trade in our tickets for a prize, the kids dumped out the shoe box on the counter with big grins and shining eyes. "What can we get?" they asked as they eyed the prizes on the wall.

The guy working behind the counter gave a smile and a half shrug. "A pencil, I guess."

"A pencil? For *all* these tickets?"

We couldn't believe it, but it was true—and the pencil didn't even come with an eraser! It was disappointing to realize that the tickets we thought we could trade in for a big prize weren't really worth all that much.

Sometimes when we do nice things for others, it's easy to think that those actions are like tickets. That somehow

we are earning points for every good thing we do, and we can trade those in for a prize with God. But here's the thing about people who are becoming love: we aren't counting our tickets anymore. Come to think of it, we aren't counting other people's tickets either.

When it comes to giving away love and grace, there aren't any tickets. We can give away endless amounts of love because it comes from God's endless supply. And we don't have to save up any tickets to buy God's love for us. He's already over-the-moon excited about us, and He fills us up with all the love we need. We can give love away like we're made of the stuff, and we don't have to keep counting tickets anymore.

16

THE LIMO DRIVER

As I rode down the escalator in the airport, I looked at the line of people waiting to greet passengers from my flight. My eyes stopped on a man wearing a fancy suit and hat who was holding a sign that said **BOB GOFF** in big, bold letters. Normally, when you see someone at the airport holding a sign like that, it means they are a driver waiting to pick up a passenger. If the driver is wearing a fancy suit and hat, it probably means they drive a fancy car, like a limousine.

To be honest, I was embarrassed when I saw the man and the sign, and I thought for a moment about just walking past. I didn't think I was cool or fancy enough to ride in a limo. But at the last second, I turned to the driver and held up my hand and gave a big wave. "Hi!" I said with a goofy grin. "I'm Bob!"

"You're Bob?" The driver looked surprised and a little disappointed. I certainly didn't look like a movie star or a professional athlete. "Who are you?" he asked. I think he was secretly wondering if I were famous.

I wanted to tell him that I'd done something really cool, like I'd invented medicine or set the world record for how many Pop-Tarts a person could eat in a day, but I didn't have anything very exciting to say. "I'm just Bob!" I shrugged.

The driver led me out to the limo, and I couldn't believe the size of the car. It was so long, it seemed to stretch around the entire block. He opened the back door for me, and I climbed in.

As we drove away from the airport, I started chatting with the driver. We talked about his family, his town, and how long he'd been a driver.

"You know, I'm really going to miss this job," he said. "I've been doing this for twenty years, and I retire next month."

Suddenly, a thought occurred to me. "Have you ever ridden in the back of one of these things?" I asked.

The driver laughed. "No, not once! I'd probably lose my job."

"Buddy, pull over the car!" I said.

And you know what? He did!

The driver scrambled around to the back of the car while I hopped into the driver's seat. After we drove a few miles, the driver said with a laugh, "This is the best ride of my life! I've always wanted to ride in the back of a limo. Now I feel like I'm famous!"

When we finally arrived at our destination and I pulled the car over, I opened the door for the man like he was about to step out onto a red carpet at an awards show.

I have a habit of carrying around medals with me

everywhere I go. They are made using a small loop of ribbon with a plastic star attached at the bottom, and it costs just a few dollars for a whole box of them! I give these medals to people to honor and celebrate them. I've given them to leaders in government offices and to the guy working behind the counter at the pizza place. I've given them to my family members, and I gave one to my friend Charlie on the side of a mountain. No matter who we are—the person riding in the back of a limo or the person driving it—we want to be seen and celebrated for the wonderful things God is making us into.

"Buddy," I told the limo driver, carefully pinning a medal to his jacket, "this medal is in honor of your years of service getting people where they need to go safely. And it's also a medal for bravery because, well, did you see how I took that last turn back there? You're fearless!"

If I'd told the driver all the things I thought he could do better or all the ways I thought he needed to change, he probably would have looked down at the ground with sagging shoulders. Instead, his chest puffed up, and he beamed with pride. He *had* served others for years! He *was* brave! When we share our love instead of our opinions, we show the love of Jesus and help others become the very best version of who God made them to be.

17

WHAT'S STILL POSSIBLE

Do you have a friend who likes to play pranks on you? I have a friend named Karl who is that friend for me. He is the kind of person who always has a fun idea up his sleeve, and he's always up for an adventure.

When Karl was young, he had a bad diving accident and hurt his neck, and now he uses a wheelchair to get around. There are times in life when we go through a loss that feels so big it's hard to imagine what we'll do next. For Karl, he had to start imagining a life without being able to use his arms and legs. All Karl had left to use, as he moved forward in life, were his mind, his heart, and his tongue. It would have been easy for Karl to believe at that point that he'd never again be able to do the things he loved, but instead Karl chose to share the things he loved with others.

While it was true that Karl would never be able to walk or dive or swim again, there was something else that Karl loved, and that was fighting for justice. As Karl healed from his injuries, he made an important decision: even though he had gone through a huge loss, he wouldn't let that stop him from helping other people.

Karl decided to go to law school, which was where we met. Karl has a quick mind and a huge heart, and he knows how to use his mouth to speak up for others. To this day, Karl is a lawyer who continues to help all types of people.

On the night we graduated from law school, Karl told our group of law school buddies that he was sending a car to pick us up. We guessed Karl was taking us to the beach for a picnic, and maybe we'd throw around a Frisbee a little. Karl hadn't given us any clues, but we knew it would be good. The car took us to a big field just north of San Diego, and in the distance we saw something bright and colorful rising from the ground.

"It's a hot air balloon!" one of my friends yelled in excitement.

We all scrambled over to the balloon basket and hopped in. Karl wasn't able to join us in the balloon, but he watched with a huge smile as the ropes tethering us to the ground were untied and we slowly rose into the sky. While Karl couldn't experience the balloon ride himself, he didn't let that stop him from sharing the experience with others. That's what people who are becoming love do—when hard things happen, they don't focus on all the things they can't do anymore. Instead, they look for what's still possible.

I've noticed the Bible talks a lot about our minds, our hearts, and our tongues. The people who wrote the Bible wrote for lots of different reasons—some parts of the Bible are written to be history books, some are written to be poetry, and other parts are written to teach. All the parts help us discover the new and different way God wants us to live. And do you know how God helps us live in that new way? By shaping our minds, our hearts, and our tongues. After I met Karl, I understood why these three things are so important and so powerful—when our minds, hearts, and tongues are shaped by God, our lives will leave a wake of beauty and purpose in the lives of those around us.

People who are becoming love let love come first in their minds, hearts, and tongues. I bet you've met people like this. They are the people who always have something inspiring and encouraging to say and who leave you feeling like you're holding a fistful of balloons when you walk away from them. They're also the people who love the things God loves, like justice and forgiveness and generosity.

If God cares so much about our minds, hearts, and tongues, we should too. Can you think of ways to share God's love with others using just these three things?

TRASH CANS

18

As you grow up, you will probably learn about all kinds of amazing people in history classes and in the books you read. You'll learn about people who invented exciting machines, accomplished incredible feats, and left the world a brighter and more joyful place. I love reading their stories.

Some amazing people, though, will never end up in a history book, but that doesn't mean their impact on the world is any less important. My friend Pat is one of those people.

When we moved into our new neighborhood, we lived just a few houses away from Pat. We quickly discovered that Pat has a really special kind of love: the kind that doesn't draw a whole lot of attention.

Pat cares about making the world a better place. Some people think that in order to make a difference in the world, you have to do something really big, but not Pat. Pat hasn't set any records or led a country or won any big awards. Instead, do you know what incredible thing Pat did? He set out our neighborhood's trash cans.

Monday was trash pickup day on our street, and every Monday, before the sun came up, you could hear the *rumble rumble rumble* of garbage cans as Pat rolled them out to the

street. Faithfully, for years and years, Pat rolled our garbage cans out to the street in the morning and rolled them back into our driveways at the end of the day. He did this for the whole neighborhood. What's amazing is that Pat never drew any attention to himself—he never mentioned the garbage cans if we happened to pass each other in the street while we were out on a walk.

Having Pat as a neighbor was like having someone in your family secretly do one of your chores for you. When I do a chore around our house, I usually want to tell everyone I know. I want to put up a sign in my yard or make a shirt that says, "I'm awesome because I mowed my lawn today!" It feels good to get attention for finishing a job we're responsible for. The incredible thing about Pat, though, is that after he took care of the chore of taking out his own garbage can, he looked down the street and realized he could help others with their chores too. Pat knew his job was to love his neighbors, so he picked a chore most people don't like—dragging smelly trash cans out to the street early in the morning—and took care of it for them.

Can you imagine how you would feel if your brother or sister surprised you by doing one of your chores for you, like making your bed or picking up your toys? I bet you'd feel pretty happy about not having to do that chore, but you'd also feel really *loved*, knowing that your sibling looked for a way to surprise you with kindness. When we treat others the way we know we would like to be treated, even with everyday things like helping to take out the garbage, we show what it means to put love into action.

Sometimes when we think about loving other people *always*, we think it means we have to do something big and splashy and exciting—something that would belong in a history book. But the truth is, God doesn't compare one act of love to another. Loving others is loving others, no matter how many people see you. Pat knew he didn't need to cross an ocean to make the world a better place—he just needed to cross the street.

I think a lot about the kinds of conversations we'll have with God when we get to heaven. I bet God and Pat will talk about trash cans and about a neighborhood that was changed because of Pat's small, consistent acts of love.

19

TIME CAPSULE

Have you ever made a time capsule? A time capsule is a jar, box, or bottle that you fill with special items and bury. The goal isn't for the time capsule to stay hidden forever, though, and when you bury it, you plan for someone—you or someone else—to discover and open the capsule years later.

When my kids were little, they decided to make a time capsule. They gathered photos of people they loved, CDs they liked, toys from kids' meals at their favorite restaurants, and a few other special items. Together, the items showed what life was like for my kids at that time.

"We need to bury this where no one will find it for years and years," Lindsey said with her most serious voice.

"I'll get the shovel!" Richard yelled.

"I'll help too!" Adam called, scampering along after him.

The kids chose a spot in the yard to bury their time capsule and started digging. Their plan was to dig a hole so big and deep that they could fit inside of it, but after a few minutes they got tired of digging. They plopped their metal box in the hole, covered it with a few inches of dirt, and—here's the funny part—they actually forgot all about it!

About fifteen years later, I was digging a hole to plant a

bush for Sweet Maria when my shovel hit something hard. *Clink!*

"What in the world was that?" I muttered to myself. I peeked into the hole and spied a shiny metal lid. When I pulled the box out of the ground and opened the lid, I was surprised and delighted by what I saw. "The time capsule! We forgot all about this!"

The kids, who were adults by that time, were delighted too. They laughed about their silly messages, trinkets, and photos. There were yo-yos, bubble gum wrappers, old CDs, drawings, and notes to their future selves. We loved discovering that time capsule so much that we decided to make it a new tradition in our family. Instead of burying trinkets and gum wrappers, though, now we bury letters—letters to our future selves and letters to other people, telling them something important about who they are and why they're loved. We don't keep the tradition to ourselves either; we invite our friends over to write letters with us!

There's something special about hiding a surprise gift for people to show them how much you love them. You might write a note to your brother, telling him what makes him such a *great* brother. Or you might write a note to your friend to share what you love most about her. Then someday, when they need it the most, you can surprise them with a map to your

buried note. They'll be amazed to learn that you were thinking about them so long ago and that you waited to tell them until the moment when they needed your words the most.

Sometimes I wonder if God does this same thing for us. Often I'll read a story about Jesus, and it will seem like the words He spoke to His friends were also words spoken to me, even though I am reading them so many years later. Has this ever happened to you? What are some words you could hide away today to surprise someone on a day when they need them the most?

20

FROM THE LIGHTHOUSE WINDOW

When I was in elementary school, my parents made me take piano lessons. All of the lessons had a single goal: to get me ready for a big recital. This was to be an important event where the lady who taught the piano lessons would bring all her students and their families together, and the students would play their songs in front of the crowd.

Another kid in my class at school took piano lessons from the same lady. His name was Greg, and he was a lot better at playing the piano than I was.

On the day of the recital, Greg played his song before me. Greg was wearing a fancy suit jacket and tie, and he looked more like the leader of a small country than a kid at a piano recital. When he sat down at the keys, Greg curled his fingers expertly, like he'd been born for this moment. He played a song called "From the Lighthouse Window," and every note was perfect. He even did the fancy piano trick where you cross one hand over the other while you play the notes.

I was up next, and I was supposed to play the same song. My knees shook as I headed toward the stage, wearing my old checkered pants and an itchy sweater my mom had bought for me.

As I sat down at the piano, I could feel everyone's eyes on me. I had practiced for weeks, and I knew all the notes to the song, but when I looked at the sea of black and white keys, I couldn't remember where to start. I decided I'd just hit some keys in the middle of the piano, and it sounded terrible. I started and stopped and fumbled my way through the song, even though I knew it so well. Something about having an audience made me freeze, and suddenly I couldn't remember any of the piano lessons and the hours of practice. Feeling hopeless and embarrassed, I put my head down on the piano keys and cried.

It was years before I touched a piano again.

When I got to college, the building where I lived happened to be across the street from the music building. Each time I passed by, I would see a beautiful grand piano sitting alone on one of the stages.

One day I passed by the music building when all was quiet inside. The door was open, and I spied the grand piano sitting in the big room, just waiting to be played. For some reason, I felt drawn to the piano. I stepped quietly into the building and looked around. No one was there.

I sat down at the piano and lifted up my hands. Here's the amazing thing: As I brought my fingers to the keys, they curled into the perfect position, just like Greg's. I began to play "From the Lighthouse Window," and this time I wasn't the kid in checkered pants and an itchy sweater who forgot all the notes. This time I hit every note perfectly. If there had been an Olympics for hitting every note in a song, I would have won the gold medal.

It turns out, all those years earlier, I'd just gotten stuck on the audience instead of the music. When I lost the audience and trusted my fingers to remember what I'd practiced, it was as if I didn't even have to think about the notes.

Whether we do it on purpose or not, we all end up memorizing the things we do over and over again. It's how God wired our brains to work. Isn't that amazing? Maybe you've noticed this when you've written your name or tied your shoes or ridden a bicycle. Even though you had to work very hard to learn how to do those things at first, after a while you could do them without even thinking. That's called muscle memory.

Muscle memory works with all kinds of things, good and bad. When you give your parents a hug and tell them you love them each night, this soon becomes a habit. If you pick on your little brother each day in the car, this can become a habit too. Because the things we say and do over and over again can start to feel natural, people who are becoming love pick words and actions that are worth repeating—things like being generous, forgiving others, and showing people we accept them for who they are.

What are some habits you would like to become muscle memory in your life?

21

WHO ARE YOU?

My jaw dropped in shock as my friends and I walked toward our rental van. All the windows were broken, pieces of glass were sprinkled on the ground, and our bags were gone.

We were in San Francisco, visiting a friend of mine who is a pastor and who gave up everything to move to a part of town where people were poor. He spent his days serving food to the homeless and showing love to everyone he met.

We had stopped by our pastor friend's house, parked the car, left our bags on the seats, and gone inside to help with chores. When we came back out, we found ourselves standing on the street, scratching our heads, wondering what on earth had happened to our bags. I needed to fly back home, so I drove back to the airport without my belongings.

The problems continued when I arrived at the airport.

"Identification, please," the ticketing agent asked when I tried to check in for my flight. I reached into my pockets to find my wallet, but it had been in my bag and was stolen too.

"My wallet was stolen out of my car today," I explained to the agent. "I don't have any identification on me, but I promise, I'm Bob. Just look at my face. Don't I look like a guy named Bob?"

The agent gave me a skeptical look. I would have been a little confused too if I were him.

"Sir, I'm going to need you to prove that you are who you say you are." I could tell the agent was starting to lose patience with me, and I understood. He was just trying to do his job keeping the airport safe, and I didn't have the identification I needed to get on the plane.

That's when I remembered that I'd written a book. I remembered it had my name on the cover, and probably a photo of me on the back cover too! I pulled out my phone to look online for a book with my picture on it, but the only thing I found was a book with a bunch of balloons on the cover. (I told myself I'd make sure to put a big picture of my face on the cover of my next book in case I lost my wallet again, but I changed my mind when I saw how funny that would look.)

Eventually, I convinced the ticket agent that I'm Bob, and I was able to fly home, but my time in the airport got me thinking about how I show others who I am. When we meet new people, we tell them our name and what we think are the most important things to know about us. This is something everyone does. We talk about something we're interested in or something we're good at. But do you know what God cares about the most when He thinks about who we are and what He says is the most important thing about us? God cares about how we love Him and how we show that by the way we love the other people He made. It's that simple.

Earlier I told you about a man named Paul who wrote letters to new churches, and some of those letters became parts of the Bible. In one of his letters to a church in a city called Corinth, Paul explained to the new followers of Jesus what love is and how important it is to show our faith in love. He told them, "If I am the best speaker in the world but I don't love other people, I'll sound like a bunch of pots and pans being banged together! And if I am the smartest person in the world and do incredible things for God, but I don't love other people, those things aren't worth anything."

What Paul wanted those followers of Jesus to understand is that our love for God and others is the most important thing about us. My pastor friend understood this. That's why he spent his time serving others. And that's what I want to be known for too. I want to spend so much time loving others that it becomes who I am, and I won't need my wallet to prove it! People will know who we are when they see how well we love.

22

BE NOT AFRAID

Our family has spent a lot of time in Uganda, which is a beautiful country in Africa full of amazing people. The first time I went to Uganda, I visited some friends who were starting an organization there and needed help from a lawyer. It was one of my first times traveling to another country, and I'm going to tell you a secret: when I got off the plane and saw a place that looked very different from the one I left, I was pretty nervous! Other than my friends, I didn't know anyone else in Uganda, and I figured I should go to a place where I might find some other lawyers: the local courthouse.

When I walked inside the courthouse, I spotted a door surrounded by lots of guards. *That must be an important judge's office*, I thought to myself.

I cautiously approached the large door and stepped past the guards into a smaller room, where I found a woman sitting at a big desk. "How can I help you?" she asked pleasantly.

"I'm here to meet with the judge," I said.

"Do you have an appointment? Is he expecting you?" she asked.

"No," I said. "But I came all the way from San Diego just to meet with the judge. Is he available?"

The woman disappeared for a moment and returned with a smile. "The judge will see you now."

I was very surprised that I got in without an appointment, but I tried not to show it. I was feeling nervous again, but I walked through another door into the back office where the judge was.

As it turned out, the judge is one of the warmest, bravest, and kindest people I have ever met. We talked for a few minutes about our shared love for Uganda, for justice, and for helping others, but do you know what we spent the most time talking about that day? Our kids!

As our time together was wrapping up, we both stood up. I walked around the desk and gave the judge a big hug. I told him I'm a hugger. He said he's not, and that's why he has guards outside his door. We laughed, and then I invited him to visit my office the next time he was in the US. I breathed a big sigh of relief as I walked out of his office, and I felt so good that I had made a new friend.

My favorite place to meet with people is on Tom Sawyer Island at Disneyland. Something about being in a special place like that, surrounded by the creativity and excitement of Disneyland, inspires conversations about things my friends and I can create too. That's why I decided that Tom Sawyer Island would be my office.

So when the Ugandan judge visited the US a little while later, I took him to Disneyland. I had Mickey Mouse ears made for him that said his nickname on the front, and he wore them as we rode the Indiana Jones ride—for his very first time! Then we went to my office at Tom Sawyer Island to talk. Our conversation quickly turned to how we could help children in each of our countries. We talked about kids who needed help in San Diego and kids in Uganda who needed safe homes and schools and grown-ups to take care of them. After that day together at Disneyland, it was hard to imagine there was a time when I was nervous to meet the judge!

Sometimes we forget to help others because we are afraid. We might be afraid of things going wrong or afraid of what people will think of us if we speak up when something isn't right. Standing up for others can be scary, and we can talk ourselves out of it. But do you know what people who are becoming love do? They ask themselves this important question:

What would I do if I weren't afraid?

Think about that for a moment. What would you do if you weren't afraid? Would you ask a new kid at your school to play with you on the playground, even if he might say no? Would you speak up if someone said something unkind about one of your friends? Would you ask your teacher a question even if you thought you should already know the answer?

The reason this is important is that Jesus doesn't want us to live our lives afraid, and He doesn't want our fears to stop us from doing the right thing. Throughout the Bible, God told His followers the same three words: *be not afraid.* That can seem impossible sometimes, but the good news is He didn't stop there—God also promises to be with us and to give us the strength we need.

23

LAND THE PLANE

You know my son Adam loves adventure and machines, and he especially loves adventures that involve machines. By the time he was twelve years old, Adam was our family's vehicle expert, both in operating machines and caring for them. Adam loved a good challenge. Could it be driven? He wanted to learn. Could it be fixed? Adam wanted to know how. Would it be a great story? Even better! "Let's do it!" were some of Adam's favorite words.

Adam turned seventeen around the time he started his last year of high school. Because he loved a challenge, Adam worked very hard early on and started his senior year already having taken all the classes he needed in order to graduate. Adam still had one year of high school left, though, so he filled his schedule with classes like art, music, and PE. Those classes were fun, but Adam and I both knew they weren't really helping him grow toward his goals—they were mostly just a way to fill his school days until graduation. What Adam really needed was a challenging project he could work on all year and that would be meaningful to him.

By that time, Adam was a great driver, and he had already mastered cars, boats, and motorcycles. What he hadn't mastered yet were airplanes. So we hatched a plan: instead of Adam taking a bunch of classes he wasn't actually interested in, we'd keep a couple of important ones on the schedule, and then Adam would leave school at noon each day. He'd head straight to the small airport near his high school and work on earning his pilot's license.

Adam stuck with it, and by the end of the year, he had his pilot's license! He even got an extra license to fly seaplanes, which are special airplanes that take off and land on water and don't need an airport with a runway. Many seaplanes don't even have wheels at all! Can you believe they make airplanes like that?

In an earlier story, I told you about the Lodge in Canada with the steep mountains that drop straight down into the ocean. There are no airports with runways nearby, so it is the perfect place to fly seaplanes. Most of the time, we take off and land seaplanes on the ocean by the Lodge.

The mountaintops near the Lodge are covered in snow, and as the snow melts in the summer, the water flows down the mountains. Some of that water makes lakes in the low places where the mountains meet each other. For years my boys and I had our eyes on one of those small lakes, wondering if it was big enough for us to land a seaplane—and then take off again.

Landing a seaplane in a lake is easy when the lake is big,

but it's not so easy when the lake is small and surrounded by cliffs. Landing in this small lake would be like landing at an airport with a very small runway, and we knew the seaplane would need to touch down on the water right at the edge of the lake, or else we would run out of space to slow down before reaching the other side.

I knew Adam had all the training and information he needed to land in this small lake, so one day I challenged him to do it. I could tell Adam was nervous, but he didn't want to walk away from a good challenge, so we climbed into the seaplane together and took off. As we neared the lake, we saw the cliffs closing in around us. I looked out the window and felt like the wing on my side of the plane might scrape against the rock wall as we made the last turn. The plane's engine grew quieter as we started to descend, and it felt like both we and the plane were holding our breaths.

Then it happened! I felt the seaplane's floats touch down on the water, right at the edge of the lake, and we came to a stop just short of the other shore. There was a moment of stunned silence in the cockpit, and then we whooped and hollered and high-fived each other. Adam had landed the plane!

After Adam landed the plane on the lake, I realized something. I hadn't given him any instructions before our flight that morning, and I didn't point out the things I would have

done differently while we were coming in for landing. It turned out that Adam really didn't need me to tell him what to do to land the plane.

Sometimes we think that loving people means constantly telling them what to do. We might do this because we want to be helpful, but other times we're scared, and we feel like we need to control what others are doing. Adam's landing reminded me that I can show others love by trusting them to do the things they're good at without my words of instruction or correction. Sometimes things will work out the way I hope and sometimes they won't, but what most people need more than instructions is love. I make a lot of mistakes myself, and I know that when I mess up, I usually don't need someone to point out what I did wrong or give me advice about how to improve—I just need a hug. That's the kind of love God wants us to show one another.

Now, this isn't to say that teaching isn't important—after all, Adam did spend a year learning how to fly airplanes from other pilots—but on the day we landed on the lake, I wasn't Adam's flight instructor. I was his dad. Adam didn't need my instructions to land the plane; he just needed me to be with him while he did it. My challenge to him that morning, and my willingness to climb into the passenger's seat, gave him the confidence he needed to try something for the first time.

As you grow up, you'll come across lots of people trying something new. Maybe they'll be learning how to read or ride a bike or paint their first painting in art class. Sometimes you'll see them make a mistake, or you'll notice something you think they could maybe do better. They might not fly a seaplane a little too close to a cliff, but they might make other kinds of mistakes, like not being polite or forgetting something important. In those moments, remember that sometimes the best way to love someone is to sit with them and encourage them, rather than correct them.

24

DIPLOMA

When you graduate from school, you get a special piece of paper called a diploma. A diploma is a certificate that says you finished your education at that school—whether it is elementary school, high school, college, or something else. It's a big honor to receive a diploma because it shows everyone that you worked hard and finished what you started.

People who earn diplomas sometimes put them in picture frames and hang them up on their walls, like trophies on a shelf, to show others what they accomplished. It's true that diplomas are something to be proud of, because school can be hard work. I know this because school was very hard for me. I had a lot of trouble focusing in class, and I had an even harder time sitting still at my desk. Does that happen to you sometimes?

When I was in elementary school, it felt like my teachers were always saying, "Bob, you need to sit down!"

"Please stop talking."

"Please don't use your pencils like they're drumsticks."

"Please finish your work."

I had a lot of energy, and that was hard for my teachers as I worked through each grade. Some of my teachers had trouble being patient with me, and I can understand that when I think about what I was like as a student.

There was one teacher, though, who never seemed to run out of patience for me. Her name was Ms. Martini, and she was my first-grade teacher.

"Bob," Ms. Martini said to me one day, "you are so full of energy that I know you're going to do great things someday. You're going to use all that energy to make the world a better place. I can just tell." She saw something in me that most other people didn't, and truth be told, it was something I didn't see in myself.

I was only six years old when Ms. Martini said those words to me, but you know what? I never forgot them. I'm a grandpa now, and I still think about Ms. Martini and what she said. It only took a few kind words to give me hope during a difficult time, when I wondered if I would ever succeed in school.

Many years and a lot of hard work later, I graduated from law school and walked across the stage to receive my diploma. I was very happy and proud, and it felt like I had just finished a long trip I started when I was a little boy. While most of my law school classmates had already ordered frames for their diplomas and were ready to hang them in their new offices, I knew what I wanted to do with mine.

I drove to Ms. Martini's house and knocked on her door.

"Mrs. Martini," I said, "you might not remember me, but I'm Bob. I was in your first-grade class twenty years ago. I just got my diploma from law school, and I want you to have it."

Sometimes we feel like we need to compete to get attention for the things we're good at, and we want trophies, awards, and compliments celebrating our successes. Wanting to be celebrated for the things that make us special isn't a bad thing, but the Bible talks about followers of Jesus being part of a different kind of competition: a competition to honor *others*. Honoring someone means recognizing how special they are. In one of his letters to a church, Paul wrote, "Try to outdo one other in the way you show honor to people."

Guess what? To this day, I still don't have an original diploma from my law school. Instead of hanging the diploma on my wall, I had way more fun showing honor to the person who deserved it most: the teacher who believed in me first and who spoke those words of encouragement and love over my life that gave me hope for my future.

Now, if you grow up and earn diplomas and decide to hang them on your wall, that's terrific! I hope you do. I know you'll remember an even more important thing though. You don't need to compete with others to win diplomas and trophies to honor yourself. Instead, the way we win in Jesus' kingdom is by honoring and celebrating others.

25

BUILD A KINGDOM, NOT A CASTLE

When our kids were little, they loved to build sandcastles on the beach. They'd build towers and tunnels, write their names with sticks, and stack rocks to make little houses for crabs to live in. Most of the time, we'd stop by the beach to take a quick walk, but before I knew it, the kids would be covered in sand as they made another terrific creation.

The sand creations always washed away as the tide rose and fell overnight, but the kids never seemed to mind. They would jump right back into building the next time we visited the beach. When the water washed away their castles and left behind a blank sheet of fresh sand, they saw it as an invitation to create more sculptures on the next trip.

Something I've noticed as I've gotten older is that lots of people spend their time building things in their lives that are a little bit like sandcastles. These things aren't *actually* sandcastles, of course, but instead they're the things we own, the jobs we have, or the things we accomplish. Like a sandcastle, these things can be beautiful and a lot of fun to work on. They can also sometimes keep us separated from other people, like

a castle with a moat. But the truth is, these trophies and cool toys and accomplishments won't last forever.

When Jesus came to live here on earth, He didn't come to build a castle. Jesus said He was here to build a kingdom. Do you know the difference between a castle and a kingdom? A castle is a building designed to keep people out, but a kingdom is an area ruled by a king, and it includes buildings and trees and people and animals and rivers and everything else you can think of. What's funny is, you don't even really need any buildings to have a kingdom. When Jesus said He was coming to build a kingdom here on earth, He didn't mean that He wanted us to each build our own castle with walls and moats to keep other people out. Instead, Jesus wanted us to join His kingdom, living together under the reign of the King and welcoming others to join. Jesus' kingdom is the kind of place you want to live.

The next time you're at the beach, I hope you stop and make a couple of sandcastles. When you do, I hope you'll also ask yourself how you can help build God's kingdom here on earth. Castles are fun to build in the sand when we understand they'll wash away, just like our trophies and accomplishments. When we build the kingdom of God, though, that's something permanent. We get to be a part of building God's kingdom here on earth by becoming love.

26

A DAY AT THE MUSEUM

Have you ever been to a wax museum? It's a place where artists make statues of famous people out of wax. Can you imagine how many bees it would take to make a whole person out of wax?

The artists form the wax to make it look exactly like a person's face, and they put in glass eyes that look real. The artists carefully attach hair and put clothes on the statues, and when you see them from across the room, you can easily trick yourself into thinking they are real people.

It's a lot of fun to look around at wax museums and take pictures with the statues. One time Sweet Maria and I decided to take our kids to one of these museums when we visited Washington, DC. I had some meetings with friends that day, so I was wearing a suit and tie, along with a long wool coat because it was cold outside.

I'm not sure who started the game, but as soon as my kids saw the statues, they wanted to pretend to be statues too. They ran around the room, striking poses next to statues of presidents and singers and athletes. They giggled as we took photos

that made them look like they were sitting at the desk in the White House or shooting hoops with basketball stars. Just as we were about to leave, I decided it was my turn. I stopped at a corner of the museum and struck a pose, gesturing with my hands like I was in the middle of giving a speech.

Just as the kids were about to snap a photo, two women walked around the corner and spotted me. "He looks so real!" one of them said in amazement, taking a closer look. "Just look at his whiskers! He's so lifelike, it's almost like he's breathing!"

At that point, I knew I couldn't break my pose because I didn't want to really scare the ladies. I held my breath in my pose and waited until they had rounded the next corner before dropping my arms and laughing. "That was a close call!" I told the kids.

We all had a good laugh about our day at the museum and my short career as a museum statue, but I actually learned something important about myself that day. I learned I'm good at pretending to be someone I'm not.

This is something we all do at times, I think. We pretend to be good at a sport when we really aren't, or maybe we make up stories about cool things we've done to impress other people. Sometimes we think the real truth about ourselves isn't worth sharing, and we think we should show others something fake so they will like us more.

The truth is, God doesn't want us to play pretend when it comes to who we are or what we believe. It's okay to be honest about what we are good at, what's hard for us, and how we feel. We don't have to pretend to be wax statues, stuck forever in the same, perfect pose. People who are becoming love know they don't need to impress other people and that, when we are honest, we let other people know that it is okay for them to be honest too.

27

THE ADMIRAL

The phone rang at two o'clock in the morning, waking me, Sweet Maria, and the kids. I woke up feeling surprised and worried, wondering why someone would call us in the middle of the night.

"Hello?" I asked in a groggy voice, trying to keep my eyes open.

"The Admiral has fallen!" the voice on the line replied.

"I'll be right there!" I replied, suddenly fully awake.

At that time, one of our neighbors was an admiral in the United States Navy. He had actually retired long before, but we all still called him "the Admiral." Something about the title seemed fitting—a special name for someone who always seemed to be in charge. During the day, the Admiral would sit on his porch and oversee the neighborhood, just like he'd overseen his fleet of ships, keeping a careful watch on the comings and goings of the neighborhood and making sure everyone was safe.

As the Admiral grew older, it became harder and harder for him to get in and out of bed at night. Sometimes, if he tried to get up by himself in the middle of the night, he'd fall and have trouble getting up. That's when I'd get a phone call, roll out of bed, and race up the street in my pajamas to the Admiral's house to help get him back in bed.

This happened often enough that the Admiral and I figured out the best way to get him back on his feet. I would lay down on the ground next to him, roll him over on top of me, give him a bear hug, then slowly stand him up. It was more than a little awkward for both of us, and the Admiral scolded me the whole time. "If you tell my men about this, you'll be in trouble, young man!" (I guess I just told you about it, but I think it's okay as long as you don't tell any of the Admiral's men.)

The Admiral became one of our good friends, and one year he was even the grand marshal of our New Year's Day parade and led the whole neighborhood down the street. Do you know why we became such good friends with the Admiral? I'll give you a clue: it wasn't because we waved when we passed each other walking down the street. The Admiral trusted us and became our friend because of the way we treated him when he fell. We didn't embarrass him or talk about his falls with others in the neighborhood. Instead, we just offered to help.

Sometimes people make mistakes and fall. They do this in many different ways. They might not get a bruised knee or scrape their elbows, but they might hurt a friend or do something embarrassing in front of their whole class at school.

Just like a person who actually falls to the ground, people who make mistakes might need help getting back up too. We show we love Jesus not by how we treat people when they're easy to love and when everything is going well but by how we treat people when they fall. What are some ways you can be there to help your friends when they need it the most?

28

KEEP YOUR EYES ON YOUR OWN PAPER

When Sweet Maria was growing up, she discovered she had a learning disability called dyslexia. This made it hard for her to read and write. Letters would get jumbled up on the paper as she tried to read them, and she stuttered when she read aloud. As Maria worked on her assignments in school, she'd often look at what the other kids were doing. They could read and write so much faster than she could.

"Why is this so hard for me?" Maria would ask herself, frustrated. It was hard to be patient with herself when she was trying her best but the schoolwork just didn't make sense.

Do you ever feel like this? It's easy to feel frustrated when we do our best but things still don't seem to work out. Maria saw her classmates finish their spelling assignments long before she did, but what she didn't see were the things in the other kids' lives that were hard for them. All Maria saw was how good they were at reading, and it made her feel bad about herself.

When we compare ourselves with others, we take our eyes off Jesus and measure ourselves by what we *think* is true about someone else. The truth is, those other people have their own struggles and things they're embarrassed about,

even if we don't see them. People who are becoming love stop watching other people to figure out who they want to be—instead, we keep our eyes on Jesus.

It was a long time ago that Sweet Maria was a fifth grader, trying to keep her eyes on her own paper, but this is still a phrase we use in our family today. If someone in our family starts to compare their life to someone else's or if they're worried that what they're doing isn't keeping up with what others are doing, we remind each other with a smile, "Keep your eyes on your own paper!" It's our friendly way of reminding each other that we aren't trying to live like the people around us—we're trying to live like Jesus. So, if you find yourself comparing your life to those of the people around you, just remember this: keep your eyes on your own paper.

29

THREE GREEN LIGHTS

I travel a lot for my job. These days I spend most of my time talking with different groups of people or visiting kids at the different schools we've started, which means I spend a lot of time driving around in rental cars or sitting in airports. I love getting to know people from all over the world, but sometimes I get a little tired from all the traveling.

One day I planned to meet a group of people in a different part of California, and at first I decided I would drive to see them. After thinking about how long the drive would take, though, I remembered something—I'm a pilot! I could rent a small airplane for the same cost as driving a car, but I would arrive at my destination a lot faster.

When I arrived at the little airport and rented an airplane, I noticed something funny—the airplane had some duct tape flapping from one wing, as if the tape were holding the wing together. The plane's paint was chipped, and the propeller looked a little tired. This was certainly not a new airplane, which explained why it didn't cost very much to rent.

When you fly an airplane, there aren't traffic lights in

the sky to let you know when to stop and go, like the ones you see when you drive a car. Instead, you talk on the radio to a person in the tower at the airport. Your job as a pilot is to let the tower know what your flight plan is, and their job is to tell you when it's safe to take off and land. When you're high up in the sky, the only lights you pay attention to are the ones on other airplanes and the ones inside your own cockpit.

The lights inside your airplane are important. Because you can't see all the parts of the airplane while you're flying, the lights tell you if each part of the plane is working properly. In my rental plane with the duct-taped wing, there were three green lights that would light up to tell me that the airplane's three wheels were lowered and ready to be used.

When I arrived at my destination and was ready to land the plane, I flipped a switch to lower the wheels and saw something that made me nervous—only two of the three green lights turned on. This meant one of two things: either one of the wheels was stuck in the airplane and hadn't lowered, which would lead to a dangerous landing, or one of the lights simply wasn't working properly. The problem was, I couldn't see the wheels beneath the plane, so I didn't know which it was!

I flew past the tower at the airport. "Hello, Tower," I called over the radio. "I only have two lights telling me that my landing gear is down. Can you see if all three wheels are down?"

I flew close to the tower, but it was starting to get dark. The air traffic controller called back on the radio, "I can't tell if you have all three wheels down. Can you fly by again?"

I flew by again, and then once more, but the answer was the same—the person in the tower couldn't see very well and didn't know for sure. I would need to land the plane without knowing if all three wheels were down.

To be completely honest, I was more than a little scared to land that plane. But as I slowly lowered the plane down toward the runway, I knew that God was with me, no matter what happened.

I softly landed on the back wheels and felt them both hit the runway. I slowly eased the nose of the plane down, praying I would feel a wheel touch the ground. To my amazement, I felt a bump! The plane gently settled onto the runway and safely came to a stop. What could have been a very big problem turned out to be nothing more than a broken lightbulb.

Later that night, I got to thinking about those two green lights, and they reminded me of something else I was learning. Sometimes, when we want to love people who are different from us, we don't know where to start. We might not know all the right words to say or how to show them our love— especially if we don't have a lot in common! Maybe you don't know exactly what to say to start a conversation with a new kid on the playground. Other times, you might not know what to say or do when someone looks or acts differently from you. When we want to love people but don't know how, it's

a little like having only two lights when you really want three.

Do you know what I've found to be really helpful in these situations? Just like I called the control tower to help me when I only had two lights, you can find safe people in your life who will be like a control tower for you. Your parents, teachers, grandparents, babysitters, or Sunday school teachers might have some great ideas for you about how to start. That's not all though. When you're worried you might try your best to show love and still make a mistake, don't forget that God is always with you—just like He was with me when I needed to land the plane!

People who are becoming love know that sometimes we need to ask for help when we want to show love to someone different, but even then, we might still have to take a risk. God wants us to move forward in loving others, even if we only have two green lights instead of three, and He promises to be with us every step of the way.

30

SLINGSHOTS AND SALTWATER TAFFY

U p at the Lodge, we only have one next-door neighbor, and it's a big one—an entire camp! The camp hosts thousands of high school students each year, and because it's surrounded by water, one of the campers' favorite activities is to go kayaking. Each morning a different group of campers gets to go on a kayaking trip, and they paddle down to a small dock by a waterfall on our property. They spend some time talking and eating bagels for breakfast, then paddle back to camp.

Every morning at 7:00 a.m., we wake up to the *thunk thunk thunk* of paddles and cheerful voices of high schoolers singing and talking as they kayak past the Lodge on their way to the waterfall. The minute I hear their voices, I run to grab my slingshot and a huge jar of saltwater taffy.

Have you ever tried saltwater taffy? It's hard for me to pick my favorite kind of candy, but I think saltwater taffy might be it. I love that it comes in rainbow colors of all different flavors.

I also love that it floats.

When the kids paddle by, I yell out from the porch, "Good morning! I have some candy to go with your breakfast!"

Then I use my slingshot to shower the paddling campers with a rainbow of taffy. It doesn't take long for their laughter to start echoing off the surrounding cliffs as they realize what's happening. "It's saltwater taffy!" they yell with delight. They paddle around in front of the Lodge, catching some taffy right out of the air and scooping up the rest from the water with their paddles.

It's a silly tradition but one that we love, and each spring I buy several huge bags of saltwater taffy to get ready for the summer. The last time I bought the taffy, I started thinking more about my morning routine of showering people with candy, and that made me wonder what it would look like to shower everyone who passes me with love. As people who are becoming love, we want everyone who walks—or paddles—past us to feel like they just got caught in a shower of kindness and encouragement.

One of the writers of the Bible talked about *devoting* ourselves to one another in love. When we're devoted to something, it means we make a plan and stay committed to it. Each summer I plan to shower campers with saltwater taffy, and I commit to that plan by filling my candy jar at the beginning of summer and rolling out of bed each morning when I hear the first *thump* of a paddle. If I want to devote myself to showering people with love the rest of the year, I need to make a plan and stick with that too.

Devoting ourselves to loving the people around us might look like shooting saltwater taffy, but it might also look like offering to share your toys with your brother or sister or read-

ing their favorite book with them. You can give smiles and hellos to your neighbors and secretly leave encouraging notes on their doors. You might write a thank-you letter to your school principal or to the fire department. You could compliment a kid at school who isn't very nice on the playground. As you go through your day, all kinds of people will cross your path. You'll get to show them how much Jesus loves them by the way you love them, and whatever that looks like, I hope you'll devote yourself to loving others in beautiful, creative ways.

31

LAST ONE, BEST ONE

I have a friend named Lex who lost his sight when he was eight years old. He had a problem with the nerves that helped his eyes tell his brain what they were seeing. Doctors tried to help fix the problem, but after several failed operations, Lex lost his eyesight completely.

This was very hard for Lex, as I'm sure you can imagine. But Lex didn't let that stop him from pursuing his dream. What he really wanted to be was a track-and-field athlete. If you haven't heard of track and field before, let me tell you what it is: it's a sport where people compete by running fast, jumping high, jumping far, and throwing far. It takes bravery, speed, and strength. I know that if I were to try track and field, I'd want to see everything clearly so I wouldn't run into anything or trip on accident. Wouldn't you? But guess what? Lex decided to keep trying anyway.

When he was in high school, Lex figured out that he was great at an event called the long jump. This is the part of track and field where the athletes have to run as fast as they can down a long runway and then jump as far as they can

into a long, narrow pit of sand. The edges of the sand pit are concrete, so if you get turned a little to the left or a little to the right down the runway and don't jump straight, you can fall and hurt yourself.

Lex was an excellent long jumper, but he had to do it without seeing where he was jumping. How do you think Lex did this? Here's his secret: he ran toward his coach's voice.

Lex's coach would stand at the end of the sand pit and call to him as he ran down the runway. When he got to the sand pit, his coach would yell, "Lex! Fly! Fly! Fly!" and Lex would leap with all his might. Lex was able to soar through the air for one simple reason. Over the noise of the stadium, there was a single voice he knew and trusted to follow.

In one of our first conversations, I asked Lex how he worked up the courage to jump without being able to see where he was going. "Bob," he replied with a laugh, "it's not about what you look at; it's about what you see." By that, Lex meant that seeing something has to do with much more than our eyes. To really see something, we need to not just look at it but pay really close attention.

The Bible tells us that until Jesus comes back to earth to make everything right, things won't always be very clear, but just like Lex, we have a trusted voice that calls our names

and wants us to run toward Him. People who are becoming love learn to know and trust God's voice and jump toward it.

Sometimes we'll get off track and fall. This happened to Lex too, especially when the crowd was loud and he stopped paying close attention to his coach's voice. We can still make mistakes even when we're trying our best to follow God's voice. Do you know what Lex told himself, though, after he fell? "Last one, best one." Isn't that great? Any time he missed a jump, he got up, tried again, and gave his last jump his very best.

God knows your name and is calling it. For the rest of your life, run toward that voice, because it's a voice you can always trust.

32

PEACE PATROL

When my kids were young, they went to the local elementary school. They liked being around their friends and learning new things, but the thing they loved most about school was the playground. The school had a huge field with soccer balls to kick, monkey bars to climb, and a slide so tall I'm sure it felt like Mount Everest at the top. (It probably wasn't as tall as an actual mountain, but you get the idea—it was awesome.)

One day the kids came home upset because of some problems they'd seen in their favorite place at school. "Dad! Mom!" they cried. "Some kids at school are starting to fight over the things on the playground!" It turned out there were a few kids who weren't sharing or being kind to other students, and the problem seemed to be growing and spreading each day. Maybe you've experienced this before too. It's hard to go to school and feel like the playground isn't a safe place, isn't it?

When problems like this come up in our lives, we sometimes want to run away from them. And the truth is, sometimes creating a little space between you and someone who is bothering you or hurting your feelings is a good thing to do. But in this case, Sweet Maria and the kids had an even better idea—rather than moving away from the kids who were being unkind, they would move toward them in love.

The kids decided to start a Peace Patrol for their school. The Peace Patrol would be a club that people could apply to join, and they'd have a special job. Every day the kids on the Peace Patrol would put on a special blue Peace Patrol jacket and walk around the playground. Their goal would be to look for ways to help other kids work out their differences. If kids were having trouble getting along or needed help figuring out how to share something on the playground, they could find a Peace Patroller to help them solve their problem. What was so great about the Peace Patrol was that the members weren't just on the lookout for problems to solve; they were also on the lookout for kids who were doing the *right* things who they could celebrate.

My daughter grew up and became a teacher, and she noticed that some of her students had the same problems she remembered from the playground when she was a kid. Her students were quick to tattle on other kids when they saw something that bothered them, instead of looking for a way to solve it.

"Kids," Lindsey told her class, "I have a new rule. From now on, unless you see someone in a dangerous spot, you can only tattle on others if you've caught them being *awesome*."

And do you know what happened? Not only did the kids start working out their own problems instead of running to her to fix them; they also started seeing all kinds of great things in one another that they might have missed otherwise.

The next time you're feeling frustrated about someone

else's actions, I want you to ask yourself, *How can I be a person who brings peace?* Jesus called these people "peacemakers," and He said that peacemakers would be called God's kids.

Sometimes being a peacemaker means overlooking unkindness and instead focusing on the best parts of other people. Other times, being a peacemaker means stepping in to help others solve their problems in a loving and creative way. People who are becoming love are always on Peace Patrol, and you don't even need a blue jacket!

33

CLIMBING BEHIND A WATERFALL

Near the Lodge is a huge waterfall that's named for the constant noise it makes: Chatterbox Falls. As you travel down the inlet, the roar and echoes sound like the waterfall is having a conversation with itself—a really loud one! All year long, water gushes down the sides of the mountains, tumbles over the waterfall, and flows into the inlet. The water comes from melting ice and snow on the mountaintops, which means it's ice cold. You can stand next to the waterfall on the hottest day of the summer and still find yourself shivering from the cold mist in the air.

One year it didn't snow very much in the mountains, and when summer came, we noticed something strange about Chatterbox Falls. With less snow to melt, the waterfall was half its normal size, and the water falling over the rocks sounded more like a library whisper than a playground yell. As my kids explored around the base of the waterfall, they noticed something they'd never seen before—there was a space in the rocks to climb *behind* the waterfall. Of course, they did what I'm sure you would do too. They asked for permission to climb behind the waterfall.

The kids were a little nervous. Even though the flow of water was smaller than normal, it was still freezing cold, and it came down so fast it was hard for the kids to keep their eyes open and see where they were going. It felt like buckets of ice water were being dumped on their heads! But slowly, the kids helped each other get past the waterfall, and I soon heard hollers of excitement from the other side. "We did it!" they yelled back to me.

Later that summer some friends visited us at the Lodge, and we decided to take them down to Chatterbox Falls. "Did you know you can climb behind it?" Adam asked the group as we got close. He and Richard led everyone to the base of the waterfall and showed them how to carefully hold on to the rocks and make their way slowly behind the curtain of water.

The rush of the icy water was overwhelming, especially because they couldn't really see where they were going. But then something beautiful happened. One by one, as our friends made their way behind the waterfall, they stopped, looked behind them, and reached out a hand to help the next person in line. Every single person walked behind the waterfall that day—even the ones who were nervous at first—and it wasn't because they were great at climbing on slippery rocks. Our friends succeeded because each one turned around to help the next person make their way through the tough spots, encouraging them that they could do it too.

The people who wrote the Bible said many beautiful things about comforting other people, but my favorite is this: God comforts us so that we can comfort others. Have you ever noticed it's easier to understand someone else's fears or sadness and comfort them when you've felt those same things yourself?

It doesn't matter if you're a kid who is six or a kid at heart who is eighty-six; we all go through hard things that feel scary for us at first. Maybe you've moved to a new city or school before, or you've felt the loss of a pet or a family member. These things are hard to pass through, but they give us a special opportunity to comfort others when they go through the same things. No matter what tough spots you go through, don't forget to stop when you get to the other side and look back to see who might need your help.

34

KIDS HELPING KIDS

There are some people in the world who see problems and say, "I can do something about that!" That's what my friend Don is like. I bet that's what you're like too.

Don cares a lot about kids having safe grown-ups in their lives who can help them grow and learn, so he decided that he would start a mentoring program for kids in a city called Portland. Have you heard the word *mentor* before? It means a trusted person who helps someone who is younger than them. What Don did was find kids who needed trusted adults in their lives to look out for them, and he introduced those kids to mentors so they could be friends.

Do you remember the earlier story where I told you about the school my friends and I started in Uganda? It's called Restore Academy, and the students there heard about what Don was doing and thought it was a wonderful idea. You see, the kids at Restore Academy have mentors too. All of the students at the school live on campus (thanks to Two-Bunk John—remember him?), and many of them are very poor and don't have families anymore. Together, they decided that they would become each other's families. Each "family" of students has a mentor, and that mentor looks after the kids.

The Restore kids know just what a big deal it can be to have a mentor who really cares about you.

Many of the kids in Don's mentoring program in Portland didn't have enough money to buy the things they needed, like school supplies or new boots for winter. Can you guess what happened next? The Restore kids heard about this problem and thought, *We can do something about that! Let's take care of the kids in Portland!* There was no way the kids at our school in Uganda were going to let a kid in Portland not have the supplies they needed for school. So the Restore kids hatched a plan—they planted extra seeds in the garden at school and sold the food they grew. Then they gave the extra money they earned from the garden to the kids in Don's mentoring program in Portland.

Just like the seeds in the garden, many beautiful friendships grew from the connection between the kids in Portland and the kids in Uganda. The biggest thing the kids have in common is that they're all becoming love. They understand that to become like Jesus, we need to love our neighbors as much as we love ourselves—even if that neighbor lives across an entire ocean! No matter where they live, when we hear someone else has a problem, we can think about the way we'd like to be taken care of in that same situation and do something to help.

Even though I'm a lot older than the students at Restore, sometimes it feels like they are the ones mentoring and teaching me about what it means to love my neighbors.

35

LIVING ON A BOAT

We sold our first house when our kids were little, but it took us a while to find another house to live in. While we looked, a friend offered to let us live on his sailboat. It was a small boat, but it had a bed in the front and a bed in the back, and our family could just barely squeeze in. We decided to go for it and make it a family adventure.

There are two parents and three children in our family, and that's a lot of people for a little boat! The thing about living on a boat is that you are always within an arm's reach of someone else. You have to get used to squishing into a tight space with other people, and you have to get used to living with fewer things. Each of us got to pick three small things we wanted to bring on the boat with us. I wonder what you'd bring with you if you could pick only three things.

What we didn't know was that living on a boat would cause some funny changes in our family. We got so used to living crammed together that even when we weren't on the boat, we ended up sticking close by each other. Trips to the grocery store looked pretty silly, with the kids clustered very close to Sweet Maria and me. Even after we moved off the boat and into a house with plenty of space to spread out, we'd often find ourselves packed into the same little room together.

What I learned from our time on the boat is that some changes in our lives happen from the inside out, but other changes happen from the outside in.

Here's what I mean: sometimes God changes things in our hearts, like helping us begin to notice people who need help or giving us more patience, and as our hearts change, the change starts to show up on the outside in our actions.

Other times, changes start on the outside, with our actions, and they end up changing our hearts. When our family moved into a sailboat and spent our time together in a small space, it changed the way we felt about each other. Living in a boat showed us how much we like being around each other, and we stayed close to each other even after our kids grew up, moved away, and started their own families.

People who are becoming love look for both kinds of changes—the inside-out changes *and* the outside-in changes. We ask God to change our hearts and teach us new things, and we take actions to give our hearts some practice.

Here's just one example: Imagine there is a new kid at school who other kids tease at recess. Maybe you've learned that Jesus wants you to love the new kid in the same way that you love yourself, but the truth is, you don't really feel very

loving, and you would rather play with your friends. If you want to become more like Jesus, start by asking Him to change your heart. Then plan a surprise act of kindness for the new kid, like inviting him to sit with you at lunch.

As you go through your day and spend time with your family and friends, check in with your heart and your actions and ask yourself, *How am I becoming love?* Is there anything on the outside or the inside that you can do to help you grow to be more like Jesus?

36

ICE CAVES

One summer day our family was up at the Lodge together, and a helicopter landed right in our front yard. I'm not kidding! We were eating lunch one minute, and the next minute there was a rush of wind and the roar of an engine as the helicopter descended through the trees and touched down on the grass. The branches on the trees waved wildly from the sudden blast of air, and all the flowers lost their petals.

We were more than a little surprised and hurried outside to see who had arrived. After all, it isn't every day that a helicopter lands in your yard, and for us this was the first time!

As we ran out onto the porch, a man in a bright blue baseball hat hopped out of the helicopter with a big grin. "Hi! I'm Deni!" he said cheerfully.

As Deni explained who he was and why he was visiting, we learned that his job was to take people on helicopter tours of the inlet. In an earlier story, I told you about all the mountains around the Lodge—the ones with tops covered in snow and ice. Each day Deni would take people on helicopter rides to see the icy glaciers on the tops of the mountains. "These mountaintops, they're beautiful!" Deni gushed. "You've never

seen anything like them. I just found a glacier with a huge ice cave inside of it. Come on, let me show you!"

A few minutes later Deni and I flew away together in his helicopter. I know it sounds a little crazy, but I could tell that Deni really loved the mountaintops, and I really wanted to see what he was so excited about.

When we landed on a glacier a few minutes later, all I could see was a giant field of white ice and snow. I didn't see any caves. Deni pointed to a small hole in the white surface of the glacier, just a few steps away. "That's the entrance to the cave," he said, handing me a helmet with a flashlight. "Follow me!"

I didn't know if I would fit, but sure enough, I wriggled through the hole and felt my feet touch the rocks below. What I saw next made me gasp. What wasn't visible from the surface was a huge maze of caves running underneath the glacier, with tunnels heading in every direction. The cave's icy walls glowed bright turquoise blue, and in the middle of the cave was a roaring river where melted water from the glacier made its way down the mountain. Looking through the transparent walls of the cave, I could see small pebbles and giant boulders trapped in the ice. It was stunning. After a few minutes, Deni and I jumped back in the helicopter to grab my kids so they could see it too.

The amazing thing about the ice caves is that they're

hidden. You could fly right over the glacier, or even stand on top of it, and never imagine the winding tunnels, roaring water, and sparkling blue walls hidden below. Lately I've been learning that people are a lot like glaciers.

When we see someone we don't know, the first thing we notice is what they look like. Oftentimes that's all we ever learn about them, because we feel like we know everything there is to know—especially if we don't think we will like them very much. Other times, a friend or family member will say something confusing or frustrating or hurtful. It's often hard to think about anything but the thing they said, and we can get stuck. Like a person standing on a glacier, all we see is a field of ice.

The Bible tells us that God doesn't look at people in the same way we do, though—when He looks at us, He sees past what's on the outside and sees what's in our hearts.

Nowadays, when someone says or does something that rubs me the wrong way, I try to think about those ice caves under the glacier. I remind myself that there is always more going on inside of a person than what I can see on the surface, just like there was a whole world of beauty I couldn't see from above the ice. Maybe the person had their own feelings hurt that morning, or maybe they're afraid of something— whatever the case, if I want to see them like God does, I need to trust that there is more to the person than what is visible on the outside.

People who are becoming love look past what most people see and get to know others' hearts, just like exploring ice caves underneath a glacier.

37

THE GREATEST LOVE

When you think of a cartoon superhero with super-powers, what do you imagine? Maybe you think about someone who can fly or who can turn invisible. I recently met some real-life superheroes, and I think their superpower is the best one of all.

There was a disease that spread across the whole world very quickly, and lots of people got sick. Because the disease could pass from person to person, it was no longer safe for people to spend time together in big groups, and people everywhere had to cancel special events—graduations, parades, parties, and weddings, just to name a few. Some of you might even remember needing to stay far apart from other people to keep them from getting sick. This was hard to do, and people gave up a lot of things that were special to them.

To stay safe, most people tried to stay away from others they knew were sick. Some people, though, did just the oppo-site. Did you know there were doctors and nurses who bravely went to hospitals every day to help those who had gotten sick from the disease? Doctors and nurses do this all the time, of course, but I bet it was especially scary when they knew it would be safer for them to stay home and that spending time close to people who were sick might make them sick too.

One day I received an email from someone who works in the emergency room at a hospital. "Bob," she wrote, "you don't know me, but I have a big favor to ask. My fiancé and I both work in hospitals, and we had to cancel our wedding because we can't get people together in large groups right now. We have been working hard to fight this sickness and we don't want anyone to get sick, but we still want to have our wedding. Is there any way we could get married in your backyard?"

It was in these two new friends that I spotted an incredible superpower—selfless love. These two people spend each day working to help very sick people get better, knowing that it might make them sick too. Even when it came time for them to get married, their first thought was about how to keep other people safe.

I thought about the idea of a backyard wedding for a moment, then had an idea. "I have a boat that's parked in the water right behind our house, like a little island," I wrote back. "What if you get married on the boat, and your friends and family can stand on the shore to watch? How about that?"

The two superheroes were thrilled, and a few days later, they had a small, beautiful wedding over the water.

One day Jesus taught His followers that they should love each other in the same way He loved them. He said, "People show the biggest kind of love when they put their friend's life before their own life." Later on, Jesus showed this kind of love for all of us when He died for us on the cross.

In my new friends, I saw the kind of powerful love Jesus talked about—a love that was willing to risk getting sick so that other people could be healed. You have probably seen this same superpower in the people who take care of you or in other heroes in your community. Even if we don't put our lives at risk, we can still practice loving people selflessly by putting their needs before our own. Every time you put someone else's life ahead of your own, you show the greatest kind of love there is.

38

MAIN STREET

If you walk down the streets of Disneyland and look at the buildings, you'll notice that some of the windows are painted with people's names and their jobs. One of my favorite windows says, "Harper Goff: Banjo Lessons." Now, I don't know Harper Goff, and even though we have the same last name, I don't think we're related. (I hope I'm wrong!) Seeing his name on a window made me curious though. Why are the windows on some of the streets at Disneyland painted with people's names?

I did a little research to find out, and here's what I learned: the windows are painted with the names of people who helped build Disneyland many years ago. Isn't that wonderful? The people who worked behind the scenes to create a special place for others are quietly celebrated in lettering on windows that most people don't even notice. I researched a little more and learned that Harper Goff was actually one of the people who created the original designs for Disneyland. What a fun job! I don't know about you, but if I helped design the main street in Disneyland, I would probably make sure to include a big billboard with my name, outlined in flashing lights.

I learned something else about Disneyland when I read about Harper Goff. Did you know there is a system of tunnels running underneath most of the park? The tunnels allow the people who work at Disneyland to get quickly from one part of the park to another, so if someone calls for help in a crowded area, others can quickly run there, underground, without having to pass by the roller coasters and castles and through big groups of people. Many of the workers at Disneyland go completely unnoticed in this way, traveling around in the tunnels and popping up to clean messes or fix broken machines.

The whole park runs smoothly because of what happens below the surface, and the people who designed Disneyland wanted it this way—they wanted to build a place where most workers would serve the guests quietly.

When Jesus taught His disciples about the new kind of kingdom He was building, many of the things He said were a

little surprising. One day Jesus told His friends that whoever wants to be great in His kingdom should serve others. I can imagine the disciples were a little confused by this because they thought great people were the ones who got a lot of attention for the incredible things they did—people who expected to be served by others and have their names up in lights. Jesus wanted His friends to understand something important though. You can't be great if you don't love others, and loving others often means serving them in quiet, unseen ways.

I've noticed that many of the people who have had the biggest impact in my life are those who live like they work in the tunnels under Disneyland. Maybe you know some people like this too. They work hard to bring joy to others behind the scenes, trying not to draw a bunch of attention to themselves. Just like the people with their names painted on windows at Disneyland, they create beautiful and extraordinary things for others and often aren't even noticed.

I don't know exactly what heaven will look like, but the Bible does say that it will have some pretty amazing streets. Sometimes I wonder if those streets will be lined with buildings, and if those buildings will have windows painted with the names of the people who helped quietly build God's kingdom—a kingdom that will be the happiest place on earth.

39

ART THE MAILMAN

When our kids were young, one of the things we loved most about our neighborhood was Art the Mailman. Art knew everyone in the neighborhood by name—even the babies! He cheerfully waved and delivered our mail every afternoon, often stopping to chat for a few minutes with our older neighbors who lived alone. If someone in the neighborhood was sick, Art would check in on them. The kids were always working on some sort of project in the front yard, and Art would stop to admire their work and ask questions, as if he had all the time in the world.

The funny thing about Art is that he often mixed up our mail, so we would open our mailbox to find letters addressed to our neighbors, and they would find ours. Art could remember when people were in the hospital, when babies were born, when someone was on vacation, and when someone new moved in, but for some reason he couldn't seem to keep our addresses straight. Every day, after Art completed his lap around the neighborhood and moved on to the next street, neighbors trickled out into the street to figure out who had received their letters and trade mail.

I have to admit that at first, Art's mistakes were a little

bothersome, but then I noticed something interesting. Art's mix-ups turned out to be an incredible gift for us, because they gave us a reason to talk with our neighbors every day! Instead of being frustrated with Art, we all loved him because of the way he cared for us and brought us together.

After many years of faithful service, Art announced that he was going to retire. "I want to spend more time with my grandkids," he told the neighbors on his last week. "I'm really going to miss this neighborhood." This made us both happy for Art and sad for us.

Our annual New Year's Day parade was coming up, and we wanted to do something special for Art to send him off to retirement in style. We asked Art if he'd be the grand marshal of the parade and lead our whole neighborhood down the street. Art was thrilled. "I'd love to!" he said with a huge smile, his chest swelling with pride. "Can I bring my family?"

The morning of the parade, Art arrived early for his grand-marshal duties wearing his mail carrier uniform, and he brought his wife and grandkids with him. Sweet Maria handed Art a box of envelopes. "These are for you to throw like confetti as you pass down the street!" We thought it would look festive and cheerful for Art to toss envelopes, and everyone on the block laughed when they heard the plan.

After the parade, all our neighbors got together to throw a surprise retirement party for Art. Everyone came to wish Art well and to thank him for the years he spent delivering our mail and bringing us together. There were toasts and cheers and claps and well wishes. Everyone could tell how happy Art was to hear about all the people he had affected.

To be honest, the next two weeks were a little boring on our street. All the letters we received were addressed to us, and it felt like we were missing something important. One afternoon, though, we heard Art's familiar whistle as he walked down the street. *Why is Art here?* I wondered. The kids cheered when they saw Art round the corner into our driveway with a handful of mail, and they asked what he was doing.

"Well," Art said, "to be honest, I had such a nice time at the parade and the retirement party that I decided to come back to work so I could see you all every day!"

Art faithfully mixed up our neighbors' mail for another five years, helping us grow closer in the process, and then he retired again. This time, he said, it would be for good. And,

of course, we asked him to be the grand marshal of the parade again that year! He said yes, and all the neighbors cheered for him once again.

Maybe there's someone in your life who makes a lot of silly mistakes, and it's sometimes hard to be patient with them. In the Bible, Paul told a church about a special way they could show love to each other—he called it *bearing* with one another. When you bear something, you hold it up. Paul wanted those new followers of Jesus to hold one another up in love, even when someone made a mistake. "Show your love through your patience," Paul wrote. "Do everything you can to stick close together, with peace as the glue."

Instead of getting frustrated and impatient with Art, our neighborhood chose to hold Art up. Instead of grumbling when we got the wrong mail, we celebrated Art for his loving service to our neighborhood. Art brought our whole community together because even though he made mistakes with our mail, he really loved us.

The next time one of your friends or family members makes a mistake, stop and ask yourself, *How can I hold them up?* Instead of losing your patience, try to find a creative way to celebrate them and hold them close.

THE OAKS GARDEN

40

Not too long ago, our family set out to plant a garden, but when we planted the seeds, we grew frogs instead of plants! Can you believe that? Let me tell you what happened.

A few months ago, one of my best friends and I bought a camp together, and we named it the Oaks. It's in California, surrounded by beautiful mountains and big, open fields.

After we bought the Oaks, we made big plans to get ready for the guests. Our first project was to create a huge garden to welcome people when they arrived. The soil in the garden has lots of clay, which is what pottery is made of, so we knew it would be hard for water to soak in when it rained. We learned that vegetables don't like to sit with their roots in water, so we made long, narrow rows to create higher spots for the plants. Even though we knew the soil wasn't the best for our garden, we decided to give it a try anyway.

My son-in-law, Jon, loves to garden, so he and Lindsey came to the Oaks one morning to help us plant. Jon carefully read the back of each seed packet to see how much sun and space each plant needed to grow, then he and Lindsey carefully planted the seeds. At the same time, our friend Justin got to work building a tall, white fence around the garden to keep out any curious and hungry animals. It took all day, but we were proud of our garden when it was planted. It took everything in me not to peek in the soil to see if we already had carrots.

A couple of weeks later we were back at the Oaks and decided to check on our garden. It had rained in San Diego that week, and we imagined all that water had probably made our plants grow ten feet tall—at least! When we drove up to the garden, though, I saw something I didn't expect. Instead of a garden full of cucumbers and tomatoes and carrots, I saw a pond full of *tadpoles*!

In case you don't know, tadpoles are baby frogs, but they don't quite look like frogs yet. They look more like tiny fish, and they swam around in our garden like they owned the place. We couldn't believe it! We planted lettuce seeds and got tadpoles instead. Then, a few weeks later, the tadpoles turned into frogs! It made me secretly wish we'd planted jellybeans to see if we could have grown giant lollipops or cotton candy trees. Wouldn't that have been great?

Did you know that Jesus talked a lot about gardening when He taught His friends about God's kingdom? One day Jesus told a story about a gardener who spread seeds on different kinds of soil. Some of the seeds landed on a road, some landed on soil full of rocks, some landed on soil that was full of weeds, and some seeds landed on good soil. Jesus said that in His

story, the soil represented our hearts and the seeds represented the good news about the kingdom of God.

"Some people are going to be like the good soil," Jesus said. "They'll hear the news about the new kingdom I'm making here on earth, and that good news will grow in their hearts and produce big changes in their lives."

"Other people," He continued, "have hearts that won't be good for growing. Some won't be ready to hear the truth about who God is and what He thinks of them, and the seed in their hearts will never even sprout. For others, the seed will start to grow, but then it will die when other things crowd it out."

When I first read Jesus' story about the gardener, I thought Jesus was trying to teach me that I should try to be good soil. When I read it again, though, I noticed something a little bit different. The gardener in the story doesn't try to change the soil to make it better, and to be honest, he doesn't even seem very worried about where he plants his seeds! Even though the gardener probably suspected the seeds wouldn't grow very well on the road or on the rocks, he spread them there anyway.

What I learned from the tadpoles at the Oaks is that gardens don't always turn out the way we predict. Sometimes we plant seeds and get carrots, and sometimes we plant seeds and get frogs.

Showing Jesus' love to others isn't always predictable either. Rather than spend our time trying to figure out whose heart is like good soil and whose is like clay, Jesus wants us to be like the gardener and share His love with everyone. We might not know for sure what they will think or what they will do, but that's okay. Whether our seeds turn into lettuce, tadpoles, or lollipops, our job is to show love to everybody, always.

ABOUT THE AUTHORS

Bob Goff is the author of the *New York Times* bestselling *Love Does* and *Everybody, Always* as well as the bestselling *Love Does for Kids*. He is the honorary consul to the Republic of Uganda, an attorney, and the founder of Love Does—a nonprofit human rights organization operating in Uganda, India, Nepal, Iraq, and Somalia. He's a lover of balloons, cake pops, and helping people pursue their big dreams. Bob's greatest ambitions in life are to love others, do stuff, and, most importantly, to hold hands with his wife, Sweet Maria Goff, and spend time with their amazing kids. For more, check out BobGoff.com and LoveDoes.org.

Lindsey Goff Viducich loves kids. She began her teaching career at a therapeutic childcare center in Seattle and went on to teach kindergarten in Nashville; first grade in Salem, Oregon; and both first and second grades in San Diego. Lindsey lives with her husband, Jon, and spends most of her free time creating art and living new stories with her family.